POLISH WINGS

Lechosław Musiałkowski

Mikoyan Gurevich MiG-19P & PM MiG-21F-13

STRATUS

Wydawnictwo STRATUS sp.j.
Po. Box 123, 27-600 Sandomierz 1, Poland
phone. +48 15 833 30 41
e-mail: office@stratusbooks.pl
stratusbooks.pl
mmpbooks.biz

ISBN 978-83-65958-06-8

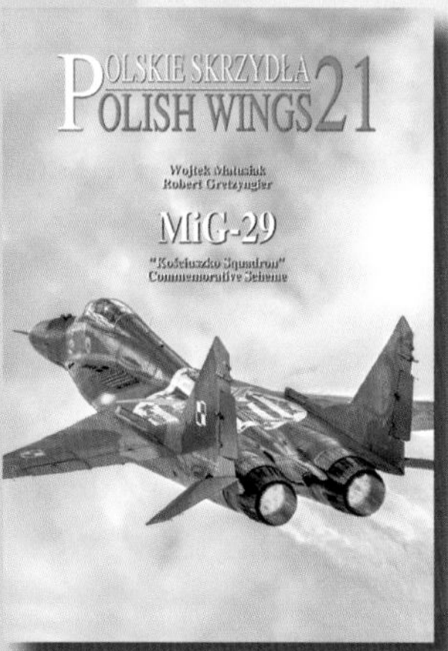

The author would like to thank the following persons and institutions for their assistance in his work on the book, and for providing photographs and documents:
Photo credits: author, Zbigniew Chmurzyński, Kazimierz Fijałkowski, Wacław Hołyś, Roman Kopras, Andrzej Lesicki, Janusz Szymański and Lech Zielaskowski.
Photographs are from archives of: author, Wacław Hołyś, Krzysztof Kirschenstein, Wojtek Matusiak, Marian Mikołajczuk, Leopold Paul, Wojciech Sankowski, Grzegorz Skowroński, Konrad Zienkiewicz, DWL Poznań and WAF.

The author would like to thank Wojciech Dubisz, Wacław Hołyś, Grzegorz Klimasiński, Wojciech Sankowski and Grzegorz Skowroński for help at various stages of work.

In memory of Janusz Szymański.

Layout concept	Bartłomiej Belcarz
Cover concept	Artur Juszczak
Cover	Marek Ryś
Translation	Jarosław Dobrzyński
DTP	Bartłomiej Belcarz
Colour Drawings	Janusz Światłoń
Edited by	Roger Wallsgrove

Wydawnictwo Diecezjalne i Drukarnia w Sandomierzu
www.wds.pl
marketing@wds.pl

PRINTED IN POLAND
Polski tekst dostępny na stronie Wydawnictwa Stratus
http://www.stratusbooks.com.pl/assets/PDF-Polskie/PW-24wkladka.pdf

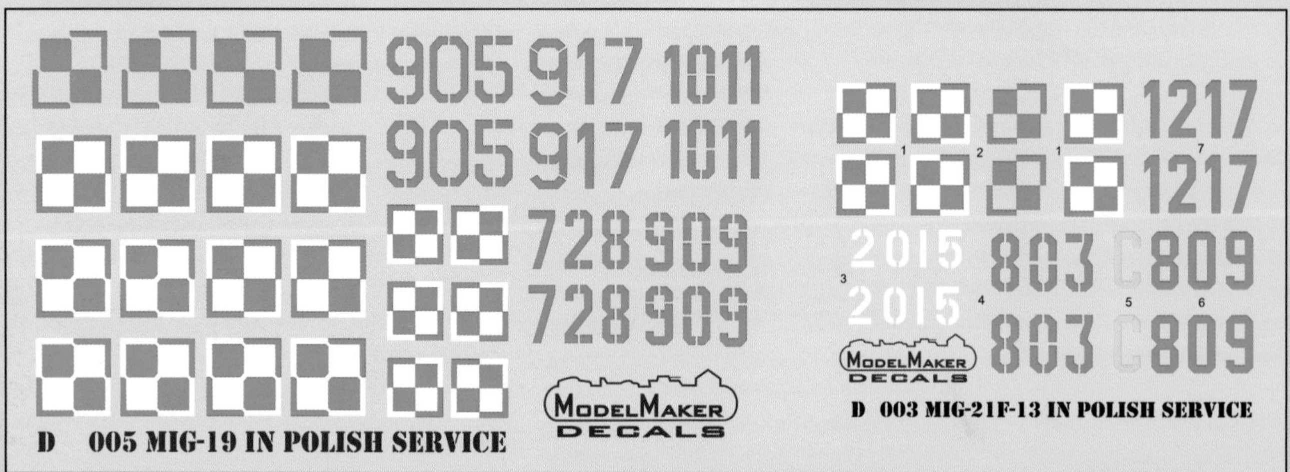

MiG-19P

The MiG-19P fighter aircraft, which appeared in Polish skies in 1958, was the first supersonic aircraft operated by the Polish military aviation. It was also the first twin engine fighter. In the USSR it was the first supersonic fighter aircraft in series production.

In military aviation the latter half of the 1950s was characterized by rapid development of supersonic aircraft, nuclear weapons and electronics. Such rapid development, never observed previously, meant that aircraft were becoming obsolete year by year or even month by month, like computer programs today. An outstanding fighter, unmatched in one year, in the next year was outclassed by a subsequent, better and sometimes avant-garde designs.

The Polish air arm saw an urgent need to have fighter aircraft with higher maximum speed and climb rate than the Lim-2 and Lim-5 then in service. Flights of NATO aircraft near Polish borders and violations of Polish airspace occurred and the air defence system proved "inadequate". The purchase of twelve MiG-17PF fighters, and later introduction of the Lim-5P fighters produced in Poland with only slightly more effective RP-5 radar, could not meet all the expectations.

In 1955 the Warsaw Pact was established and then the Headquarters of United Armed Forces of Warsaw Pact Member Countries. After the events of June 1956 in Poznań the transformations in October 1956 in Poland led to significant changes in the Polish Army, including the Air and Aerial Defence Forces. Brig. Gen. Jan Frey-Bielecki was appointed the new commander. A major revision of the organizational structure and training system was made. From detached tactical units of aviation, antiaircraft artillery, observation and reporting troops, three air defence corps were formed. These corps were tasked with defence of assigned sectors, which approximately matched the areas of individual military districts. The Warsaw Military District cooperated with the 1st Air Defence Corps, the Pomeranian Military District with the 2nd Air Defence Corps and the Silesian Military District with the 3rd Air Defence Corps.

The necessity of possessing supersonic interceptors was seen and plans to purchase such aircraft were developed. Obviously the USSR, where in 1954 production of MiG-19S fighters began, could be the only supplier of such aircraft for the Polish air force. In 1955 the MiG-19P (*izdeliye* 62) and two years later the MiG-19PM (*izdeliye* 65) made their first flights.

[1]: Take-off of a pair of MiG-19P fighters, "728" and "723", from Mierzęcice air base.

[2]: Aft fuselage and tail section of the MiG-19P "721". Serial number N670721 is visible on the vertical stabilizer and rudder. In the background ground crews maintaining the TP-19 brake chute are visible. The photo was taken at Mierzęcice air base, home of 39. PLM.

2

3

[3]: MiG-19P "721" visible in the background at Nowe Miasto airfield in 1964. The aircraft undergoing maintenance in the foreground has the tip of the PTB-760 underwing fuel tank dented and painted white. RV-2 radar altimeter antenna is visible under the wing.

[4]: MiG-19P interceptors "723" and "1015" on the runway of Nowe Miasto airfield. RP-5 radomes on both aircraft are painted gray.

4

The decision to equip the Warsaw Pact member countries with MiG-19S, MiG-19P and MiG-19PM aircraft was made in the USSR. Beginning implementation of the process was scheduled for 1957, after signing contracts between the USSR and Bulgaria, East Germany, Poland and Romania. The contracts also included training of assigned air and ground crews. Czechoslovakia purchased a licence for MiG-19S fighter production from the USSR. The fighters licence-built at Vodochody were designated S-105.

Poland did not purchase and operate MiG-19S fighters. For decades, when everything in the Polish Army was secret, obtaining and publishing information about the number, types of operated aircraft and their technical specifications was impossible. Therefore several speculations and fantasies appeared. False information appeared in four Polish publications, in which in the 1980s MiG-19S tactical numbers "711" and "916" were given. They also included colour profiles of these aircraft with Polish markings. This was not deliberate disinformation. Also incorrect was the information about six Polish MiG-19S aircraft with tactical numbers "212", "219", "1623", "1626", "1722" and "1725", given along with false serial numbers by a Russian author, in a book issued by Midland Publishing of Great Britain in 2003.

Polish military authorities decided to purchase 36 MiG-19 aircraft of the two latest versions. Of these 24 were MiG-19Ps and only 12 MiG-19PM aircraft. On one hand the higher cost of purchase of the MiG-19PM and its missile armament was taken into consideration. Also taken into consideration was the fact that, in case of powerful electronic countermeasures by the enemy, the missiles being the only armament of the MiG-19PM would have not be effective against aerial targets. Larger numbers of MiG-19s of both version were not purchased because it was expected (precipitously, as it turned out) that MiG-21 new generation fighters, whose prototypes were then undergoing evaluation in the USSR, would be acquired soon. The contract stipulated conversion of two Polish pilots on the new type in Krasnodar.

Two pilots of the 21st Independent Fighter Squadron (21. SELM), Captains Czesław Kantyka and Zdzisław Mickiewicz, were sent for conversion in the USSR by the Air and Aerial

5

[5]: MiG-19P "723" as the background of an occasional photograph taken at Wrocław-Strachowice airfield.

[6]: MiG-19P "723". AKS-3M and SSh-45 gun cameras mounted in a single fairing on the right side of the air intake are visible. Mounted below the inspection hatch is the TP-156 air data probe. The number 0723 is visible on the gun barrel fairing.

[7]: MiG-19P "724". Two of three wheel well covers and PTB-760 underwing tank pylon are visible.

6

7

Defence Forces headquarters. They underwent theoretical and practical training in the USSR in 1956–1957. In early 1958 conversion of three pilots of 21. SELM, who were to form the instructor staff for the future Advanced Flying School, began. These were Capts. Janusz Jadczuk and Stanisław Radziejowski and 1st Lt Roman Operacz. To prepare the base for establishment of a national MiG-19 conversion center for air and ground crews in Modlin, the units of the 15th Bombardment Division were moved from Modlin to Powidz. The 38. PLM (38th Fighter Regiment) was moved to Modlin from Powidz and merged with the 21. SELM, forming a new type of training unit, *Wyższa Szkoła Pilotażu* (Advanced Flying School) in 1958. The Polish air force's entry into the supersonic era required training of a large number of specialists. Training them in the USSR would have been very expensive and impossible, both timely and organizationally. Implementation of this task was scheduled for the spring of 1958 to coordinate it with the entry of the new MiG-19 fighters in service. The completion of deliveries of 36 aircraft of all versions was scheduled for 1960. The aircraft were to be delivered by train to Warsaw Babice (Bemowo) airfield. This airfield had a couple of hangars, proper infrastructure for stationing aircraft of this type and two runways. In one of the hangars, belonging to the 1st Aerial Defence corps, the assembly facility for the delivered aircraft was established. Along with the aircraft, a group of factory technicians for assembly and pilots arrived in Warsaw. From October 1957 the aircraft were assembled by the technicians and flown by the manufacturer's pilots. After the test flights the aircraft were formally handed over to the representatives of the Polish air force.

The first batch of eleven MiG-19P fighters commissioned on 3 December 1957 was deployed to Modlin. These were aircraft of the 7th production batch, with serial numbers 62210721, 62210723, 62210724, 62210726, 62210727, 62210728, 62210729, 62210730, 62210734, 62210736 and 62210739. In the eight-digit serial numbers the first two digits

8

[8]: Pilots of the 1st Squadron of 39. PLM based at Mierzęcice. Sitting on the wing are Captains M. Furmanek, W. Niedbała, E. Witkowski and M. Sygnowski. Standing in front of them are, from left, 1st LT J. Parkitny and Captains Z. Pardela, L. Paul, T. Perlikowski, D. Wilkin and M. Matanóg. Small number "728" is painted on the fuel tank.

9

[9]: ORO-57K launcher for eight S-5M unguided rockets under the wing of the museum display aircraft "728". Open airbrake is visible.

[10]: MiG-19P "728" preserved at Polish Arms Museum in Kołobrzeg. The air intake cover is from aircraft "1017".

10

(62) denoted the MiG-19P product code. The next two digits (21) were the number of the production plant – Gorki. The last two digits denoted the production batch (07) and individual aircraft of this batch (21). Tactical numbers of Polish MiG-19s were equivalent to the last four digits of the serial number. The numbers were three-digit when the first of four digits was 0. In May 1958 a group of a dozen or so pilots were assigned for MiG-19 conversion. They were pilots from the 21. SELM, 28th (Air Defence) Fighter Regiment (28. PLM OPL) in Słupsk, 39th (Air Defence) Fighter Regiment in Mierzęcice and 62nd (Air Defence) Fighter Regiment in Poznań-Krzesiny. After conversion they were to comprise the first group of pilots of the interceptor squadrons. Initially, in the period of preparation for supersonic fighter conversion, they qualified in MiG-17PF fighters, fitted with RP-1 radar. As with the MiG-17 there was no two-seat trainer version of the MiG-19 in the USSR, so neither was there in Poland. It required from the instructors at Modlin more attention and time for training future pilots of supersonic fighters. (The two-seat version of the MiG-19S, designated JJ-6, was developed and produced in China. Under the designation FT-6 it was exported to Albania, Bangladesh, Egypt, Pakistan, Somalia and Tanzania and Vietnam). As early as the first half of May 1958 th first exercises, consisting of take-off runs on the runway, were conducted. The trainees gradually progressed to subsequent cycles of exercises, including simple elements of flight, such as take-off runs, enabling the pilot to become acquainted with the dynamics of acceleration of the fighter with two engines running, take-offs, flights in the circuit pattern and landings. The training was completed on 20 September 1958. Simultaneously a group of technical specialists from selected units was trained. A second batch of 13 MiG-19P fighters was delivered to Babice airfield by rail. After being assembled by technicians and flown by manufacturer's pilots they were delivered to the Advanced Flying School in Modlin. On 17 May 1958 the ground crews accepted for the School's inventory MiG-19P aircraft of the 10th production batch, with following serial numbers: 62211007, 62211008, 62211011, 62211012, 62211015, 62211017, 62211018, 62211021, 62211023, 62211024, 62211025, 62211027 and 62211029.

MiG-19P fighters of the 10th production batch differed from the eleven aircraft of the 7th production batch from the previous delivery. In MiG-19P aircraft of the second batch the dorsal fairing, covering the electric and antenna wire bundles, was taller and broader than in the fighters of the seventh batch from the first delivery. Its junction with the horizontal stabilizer base was smooth, without distinct division of the skin's sheet metal panels. The base of the vertical stabilizer was taller than that of the aircraft of the 7th batch. Similarly smooth was the transition of the canopy into the dorsal fairing. Since the dorsal spine was taller and broader, the shape of the gasoline and kerosene filler inspection hatch access panel, located on the port side aft of the sliding canopy fairing, was changed.

After the acceptance of the second batch of the new aircraft all the purchased MiG-19P fighters were in the inventory of the Advanced Flying School.

The MiG-19P was a new quality in comparison with previous Polish fighters. While the MiG-17F and its versions produced in Poland were developed as extensive modifications of the previous type MiG-15bis, retaining its general configuration and similarity in shape, the MiG-19 was an entirely new design. The new quality was also visible in the price of the aircraft. Its predecessor, MiG-17PF cost 5.07 million zloty and the price of the MiG-19P was 12.596 million zloty.

The MiG-19P was fitted with RP-5 (*Izumrud* series) radar. The RP-5 (RP for "*radiopritsel*", targeting radar) was more reliable than the RP-1, was mounted on twelve MiG-17PF fighters of the 21st production batch, purchased for the Polish air arm. The RP-5 radar enabled operations in poor weather, detecting targets in the forward hemisphere of the aircraft and homing on the target with the use of the cursor on the radar scope. It was a two-antenna radar. In the upper part of the air intake the antenna of the target search system was mounted under a dielectric fairing. In the intake, in the middle of the inlet duct splitter wedge, the antenna of the target tracking system, faired over with a conical radome, was mounted.

11 *[11]: MiG-19P "730" during a take-off roll. Contrary to appearances this photograph is not faked. Janusz Szymański took this photograph with artistic emphasis of the speed of the fighter taking off.*

The search range declared by the manufacturer was 12 km and the tracking range was 2 km.

Numerous new methods were employed in the design of the MiG-19P interceptor. Circular section of the forward section of the fuselage was gradually merged to the elliptical going rearwards, to accommodate two axial-flow turbojet engines side by side. Previous Polish jet aircraft had centrifugal-flow engines. One of the advantages of the axial-flow engines was their smaller diameter, enabling a side-by-side arrangement of the engines in the aft fuselage section with maximum diameter of 1,450 mm. In the MiG-19P, as in the previous versions there was no gun platform beneath the forward fuselage, as in the MiG-15 and MiG-17 fighters. Axial engine compressor stalls when firing guns mounted under the nose or in the inlet duct

12

13

[12]: MiG-19P "734" operated by 28. PLM OPK based at Słupsk from 1961. It was lost in a crash at Strzepcz bombing range on 17 June 1970.

[13]: MiG-19P "736" used as technical aid in the Air Force Technical Officer Training School in Oleśnica.

[14]: MiG-19P "739", operated by the Air Training Centre at Modlin in 1960, piloted by Capt. Tadeusz Góra, after an emergency belly landing. After repair the aircraft returned to service. It was written off after another accident on 19 September 1972, during service in 28. PLM OPK. The wheel brakes failed during taxiing after landing and the aircraft collided with obstacles near the taxiway.

14

splitter occurred in MiG-9F jet fighters. When the guns fired at high altitude, both engines flamed out. Initially it was thought that after opening fire the engines flamed out at high altitude due to lack of oxygen, "suffocated" by the propellant gases of the 37 mm cannon, mounted in the middle of the air intake. It turned out later that the true reason for the flameouts was different. It was concluded that hot streams of propellant gases caused thermal and aerodynamic heterogeneity on the blades of the axial engine compressor. Moreover variable heavy loadings occurred on them, being the direct cause of the engine flameout. It was a compressor stall phenomenon. In the MiG-15 and MiG-17 there were no such problems, because their engines had centrifugal compressors. The problem returned when the powerplant of MiG-19 fighters comprised RD-9 and then RD-9B engines with axial compressors. Due to known the vulnerability of axial flow turbojets to thermal heterogeneity of the airflow, the most convenient way of installing cannons on a platform beneath the forward fuselage was abandoned. Two NR-30 cannons with a rate of fire 900 rounds per minute were installed in the wing roots. 30 mm ammunition (73 rounds) was housed along the leading edge. The employment of 30 mm cannons in MiG-19S and MiG-19P fighters resulted from research into optimal calibers of aerial cannons for various purposes, conducted in the USSR in the early 1950s. It was decided that the best caliber of conventional automatic cannons for fighter and fighter-bomber aircraft was 30 mm.

The MiG-19P could carry four ORO-57K launchers with eight S-5 57 mm unguided rockets to attack ground targets. Two were carried under the wings on inboard pylons on the rear sections of the wings, ahead of the wing flaps. Additional two such launchers could be carried on universal underwing pylons with BD-3-36 ejector racks in lieu of fuel tanks. The MiG-19P could also carry two 50–250 kg bombs on two universal pylons in lieu of fuel tanks. An ASP-5N sight, coupled with the RP-5 radar, enabled accurate bombing and firing of unguided rockets from ORO-57K launchers.

To the wings, swept at 55°, 32 cm tall wing fences were attached on each wing to prevent span-wise airflow along the wing and abrupt flow separation at high angles of attack. To increase effectiveness of the ailerons and improve control along the roll axis at high speeds, spoilers were installed on the lower surfaces of the wing, deploying automatically to the height of the boundary layer to boost lift. The spoilers were coupled with the aileron control mechanism. The spoiler was deployed only on the wing whose aileron was deflected down at angles exceeding 3°. The spoiler deployed fully when the aileron was deflected at 8°. When the aileron was in the neutral position or deflected upwards the spoiler did not deploy.

The MiG-19P, like the MiG-19S, was fitted with all-moving tailplanes (stabilators). This horizontal empennage configuration was resistant to aerodynamic blockage at high speeds. The stabilators had 8.2 kg anti-flutter weights attached to the

15

16

[15–16]: Two staged photos next to MiG-19P "1008", taken in 39. PLM OPK at Mierzęcice.

17 *[17]: MiG-19P "1008" with open engine access hatch.*

tips. Control was assisted by a hydraulic booster, doubled with an APS-4 electric mechanism, which engaged automatically when the pressure in the hydraulic system dropped below 50 kG/sq.cm. The MiG-19P was also equipped with the ARU-2V automatic control regulation system, altitude-corrected to 15,000 m. This automatic system made the pilot feel stick forces depending not only on the stick deflection, but also airspeed and altitude. Despite this entirely new flight control system, flying the MiG-19P aircraft was compatible with habits acquired on subsonic aircraft. Since the MiG-19P aircraft had the stabilators attached to the fuselage rather than the vertical fin (as on the MiG-15 and MiG-17) the lateral air brakes were relocated. The objective was to avoid dangerous effect of the deployed brakes on airflow around the empennage. Thus they were located beneath the fuselage's longitudinal axis, where the vortexes generated by them did not spoil stabilator action. The MiG-19 aircraft (from the MiG-19S version) were fitted with a third airbrake beneath the fuselage, which reduced vibration and pitching moment, caused by underpressure generated behind the airbrakes and stabilators. The rudders of Polish MiG-19P

18

19

[18–19]: MiG-19P "1011" operated by 28. PLM at Słupsk. Note different shape of the tactical number digits, and checkerboards painted with a different stencil. On the port side of the fuselage the open brake chute container is visible, next to the ventral fin.

[20]: Parade formation at Nowe Miasto air base in 1964. All 16 MiG-19s which demonstrated the "arrowhead" formation are visible in the photo. ZiŁ-164 trucks with ground power units supply power to the aircraft. Last on the right is "1012". In this aircraft 1st Lt Roman Operacz officially broke the sound barrier for the first time in Poland. It was operated by 28. PLM at Słupsk till 1967. On 16 June 1967 the forward fuselage section of this aircraft was destroyed when it was hit by a Gacek *aerial target, after the tow line was cut from an Il-28 aircraft from 19nd Tow Squadron at Słupsk air base.*

20

21 *[21]: MiG-19P "1015", Nowe Miasto air base, 1964.*

22 *[22]: Take-off of MiG-19P "1015". This aircraft was operated by 28. PLM until an accident caused by pilot error on touchdown and landing on 22 January 1971. The aircraft was written off in November 1971.*

23 *[23]: MiG-19P "1017" operated by ATC Modlin. From 1962 it was operated by 28. PLM OPK at Słupsk. On 3 December 1974, the day of the final flight of MiG-19 fighters in Polish service, this aircraft was damaged on landing because the nosewheel failed to lower.*

[24]: MiG-19P "1018" displayed as an exhibit in the Air Force Technical Officer Training School on the apron of Oleśnica airfield. The radome is not in original paint.

fighters had no movable trim tab, only the fixed rudder tab. The MiG-19P and PM fighters were the first aircraft in Poland equipped with brake chutes. The TP-19 brake parachute was housed in a container on the port side of the ventral fin. The parachute, 15 m^2 in area and 4.5 m in diameter, after deployment generated a pitching moment, pressing the nosewheel to the surface of the runway and increasing the wheel brake effectiveness.

The new egress system, rescuing the pilot in an emergency situation, was the KK-2 ejection seat. To avoid hitting the vertical fin in flight at high speed, a propellant charge was used, in which after firing the explosive the rocket motor was engaged. The action of the propellant charge enabled the KK-2 seat to climb to a higher altitude without exceeding permitted g forces. In case of low altitude ejection the seat climbed to higher altitude to enable the parachute to deploy. There was another new factor in the MiG-19P's egress system. When the pilot was not able to jettison the canopy before ejection, the armored headrest of the seat penetrated through it. The minimum ejection altitude was 250 m. To ensure the pilot's security in case of cockpit depressurization or ejection at high altitude, the pilots were equipped with partial pressure suits. When necessary, the hoses of the pressure suit were inflated with oxygen from a bottle within 2.5–3 seconds. They squeezed pilot's body, creating pressure equal to the pressure in the pilot's lungs, enabling regular breathing and blood circulation. The pilot's suit was complemented with a helmet with oxygen mask.

The two PTB-760 underwing fuel tanks had larger capacity than those previously used on Polish fighter aircraft, containing 760 liters of fuel each. The MiG-19P in clean configuration, without underwing fuel tanks, attained a speed of 1,432 km/h with afterburner at 11,000 m.

The first combat unit to which the MiG-19P fighters were assigned, in the autumn of 1958, was 62 PLM OPL (62nd Air Defence Fighter Regiment). The regiment CO's order of 11 August 1959 to form the 1st Pursuit Squadron within the 62. PLM at Krzesiny reveals that the squadron had eight MiG-19P aircraft. No. 1 Flight received aircraft with tactical numbers: "724", "728", "734" and "1011", No.2 Flight had four aircraft: "721", "723", "726" and "1008". There is no confirmation in official sources that MiG-19PM fighters were operated at Krzesiny.

In 1958 the first MiG-19P fighters were assigned to the 1st Squadron of 39. PLM OPL at Mierzęcice.

Later, in early December 1958, four MiG-19Ps were flown from Modlin to 28. PLM OPL at Słupsk. Aircraft with tactical numbers "727", "729", "730" and "736" entered the Regiment's inventory on 2 December 1958. A number of aircraft was still in the inventory of the Advanced Flying School at Modlin, where further pilots were trained. The MiG-19Ps from Modlin participated in displays and parades. The instructor pilots from Modlin trained new pilots on the supersonic fighters and took part in numerous displays and parades. The number of aircraft in the inventories of combat units operating the MiG-19Ps and AFS varied. The aircraft were sent for overhauls to Plovdiv, Bulgaria.

In July 1958 during the flight training of the first group of pilots, the headquarters of the Air and Aerial Defence Forces organized a display of MiG-19P fighter capabilities for state and military authorities at Babice airfield. The display pilot was the commander of the 1st Interceptor Training Squadron of the AFS at Modlin, Capt. Czesław Kantyka. In order to make the display for the officials impressive, it was preceded by several rehearsals. During the display, after several passes at various altitudes, the aircraft broke the sound barrier in level flight. It was the first time that the sound barrier was broken and the sonic boom sounded in Poland. The first public display of MiG-19P supersonic fighters took place during a great military parade on 22 July 1959, organized on the occasion of the 15th anniversary of the People's Republic of Poland. Apart from other attractive parade formations, the display of the new fighters was the most impressive moment, ending the air parade. In the fast fly-by the aircraft were piloted by Capt. Czesław Kantyka, Capt. Bogusław Jaromin, Capt. Zdzisław Skrzydłowski, Capt. Zdzisław Mickiewicz, 1st Lt Jerzy Makarewicz and 1st Lt Jerzy Ociepko. After 30 seconds another MiG-19P ("1012"), piloted by 1st Lt Roman Operacz, demonstrated the breaking of the sound barrier. Training for the display was conducted during parade training at Babice airfield. Before the supersonic flight display the profile of the planned flight was tested. Due to breaking of the sound barrier at high altitude being unimpressive, one rehearsal was conducted at much lower altitude. The effect was attained, the boom was so loud that window panes in houses near the airfield were smashed. It was then decided to have a less harmful effect and the altitude and profile of flight was changed. For the next time the MiG-19P fighters were displayed at the harvest festival, held at Decennium Stadium in Warsaw. It was honored with an air show, and the final event was a fly-by of two MiG-19P fighters from 28. PLM OPL. The first one, piloted by Capt. Franciszek Koźlak, made a low pass and the other one, piloted by 1st Lt Władysław Barański, broke the sound barrier at an altitude of 7,000 meters above the stadium.

During a technical test flight of a MiG-19P fighter after routine maintenance, in the latter half of 1959, the first air accident at the Flying Training Centre at Modlin occured. The flight was made by 1st Lt Roman Operacz. During maneuvering at 3,100 m an ammunition belt inside the wing broke loose and damaged the relay of the flight control boost system. The stabilator control system switched from high to low speed, causing oversteering. Thus a small move of the control column caused rapid attitude changes, from nearly vertical climb to steep dive. The aircraft and pilot were subject to g forces from +10 to – 5. The seat belts ripped off, which led to injuries to 1st Lt Operacz. Despite his injuries the pilot managed to bring the situation under control and land. The aircraft required overhaul. First Lieutenant Operacz was taken to hospital and recovered quickly. For saving the aircraft he was awarded with the Air Force dirk with proper dedication by the CO of Air and Aerial Defence Forces.

On 30 June 1960 at the Air Training Centre an engine failure occurred in the MiG-19P "739", taking off in three-ship formation for a training flight before a display over the fields of Grunwald. Just after liftoff one of the engines quit, followed shortly after by the other one. Capt. Tadeusz Góra made a masterpiece off-field emergency belly landing. Slight damage to the aircraft, that skidded 700 meters on grass, was repaired. The engines were replaced and within a fortnight Capt. Góra flew this aircraft again.

The Modlin pilots demonstrated the MiG-19P aircraft in the air on 17 July 1960 over the fields of Grunwald, on the occasion of the 550th anniversary of victory in the battle with the Teutonic Order. However, they performed in a different formation, the so-called parade formation or five-ship stream. The formation, codenamed "Delta", flying at the altitude of 100 meters and

[25]: MiG-19P "1021" as background to a commemorative photograph taken in the 28. PLM in 1970, after winning the prize in an aerial reconnaissance competition.

25

speed of 1,000 km/h, was led by Capt. Zdzisław Mickiewicz, followed by Capt. Tadeusz Góra, Capt. Stanisław Radziejowski, Capt. Henryk Danko and 1st Lt Stanisław Chreptowicz in the slot position. Thirty seconds later 1st Lt Roman Operacz made a high-speed pass at 6,000 m, breaking the sound barrier, which was heard as a characteristic boom. In 1960 the MiG-19P aircraft were again displayed in public during an aviation day at Lublinek airfield in Łódź on 11 September. This time a three-ship formation made a low-altitude pass at 1,000 km/h. As previously, the display was spectacularly ended by 1st Lt Roman Operacz breaking the sound barrier, which became his airshow specialty.

In early 1961 at the Air Training Centre (renamed from Advanced Flying School after reorganization in 1960) the last group of pilots qualified in the MiG-19P and in the spring the "nineteens" began to be transferred to combat units, to prepare the 1st Air Squadron of the Air Training Centre for reception of MiG-21F-13 fighters. The MiG-19Ps were in the inventory of the 1st Squadron of 62. PLM OPL at Krzesiny only until 1962, because the Poznań regiment was soon to be equipped with MiG-21F-13 fighters. In September and October 1962 MiG-19P aircraft were transferred from the 62. PLM to the regiments based at Słupsk and Mierzęcice.

In March 1962 the MiG-19P 1029, previously operated by Advanced Flying School at Modlin, was written off the inventory of 28. PLM. The damage, sustained on landing due to brake system failure, was so extensive that the aircraft was scrapped.

In April 1963 the 1st Squadron of 39. PLM operated the following MiG-19Ps : "721", "724", "726", "727", "728", "730", "1012", "1023", "1024", "1025" and MiG-19PMs: "910", "911", "912", "914" and "917".

In the spring of 1964 preparations for the air parade over Warsaw on the 20th anniversary of the People's Republic of Poland began. On 22 July the formation, codenamed "Lambda", was demonstrated over the Parade Square. It consisted of 20 MiG-19P and MiG-19PM aircraft, flying in four five-ship Vee flights. The aircraft and crews (10 plus one spare aircraft each) were provided by 28. PLM OPL and 39. PLM OPL. The entire formation and first Vee flight were led by Maj. Marian Kawczyński of 28. PLM at Słupsk. The following flights were led by Capt. Alojzy Zgondek, Capt. Czesław Brzozowski and 1st Lt Władysław Waltoś. Last two flights were from the 39. PLM based at Mierzęcice. The "Lambda" formation flew over the tribune at an altitude of 350 m and speed of 850 km/h. In 1966 a great parade with Air Force participation was held on 22 July, on the occasion of the thousandth anniversary of the Polish state, merging the beginning of the state of Prince Mieszko I with the July date of the start of Sovietization of Poland in 1944. For the display of supersonic aircraft, apart from the new MiG-21 and Su-7, MiG-19 crews were also committed (16+2 spare pilots). In the echelon of supersonic aircraft, comprising MiG-21s, plus sixteen MiG-19Ps and MiG-19PMs 28. PLM at Słupsk and 39. PLM at Mierzęcice. The "Arrowhead" formation, consisting of the "nineteens", like the "Arrowhead-Centre",

26

[26]: A beautiful photograph of MiG-19P "1024" in flight.

27

[27]: MiG-19P "1024" during its service in the 28. PLM.

[28]: A commemorative photograph with MiG-19P "1024". Standing third from left is Capt. Tadeusz Góra, a famous glider pilot, who during the Second World War was a fighter pilot in the Polish Air Force in Great Britain.

"Arrowhead-Pomerania" and "Arrowhead-North" formations consisting of MiG-21 fighters, was demonstrated for the first time then. Each sixteen-ship "Arrowhead" formation was composed of a quartet of four-ship "arrowheads".

On 24 August 1964 at 39. PLM at Mierzęcice, the pilot of the MiG-19P "727" made an error, performing an overshoot landing. The brake chute failed to deploy. Violent braking was not sufficient and the aircraft overran the runway and was only stopped by the arresting net. Nose landing gear and radio were damaged. The airplane was repaired and returned to service, but only for two years, as it turned out later.

On 3 August 1966 a fatal crash occurred during night flights by the 39. PLM. The MiG-19P "727" was lost due to asymmetric thrust, when one engine lost power on take-off with afterburner from the reserve airfield at Kamień Śląski. Capt. Eugeniusz Nasierowski was killed. During 1966–1967 the MiG-19Ps were transferred from Mierzęcice to Słupsk. The last two sorties on MiG-19Ps in the 39. PLM were made by Capt. Władysław Waltoś on 6 May 1967. Thus the 28. PLM became the only operator of the "nineteens" in Poland.

On 16 June 1967 the MiG-19P 1012 was written off the inventory of the 28. PLM at Słupsk. It was scrapped when a Gacek aerial target hit "1012" standing on the flightline, destroying its nose section, after the line had been cut by the Il-28 tug aircraft. Another MiG-19P in the Słupsk regiment was lost on 11 February 1970. During a night flight there was an explosion and engine fire in "1007". The pilot managed to eject safely.

Four months later, on 17 June, a fatal crash took place in the 28. PLM. It happened at Strzepacz bombing range, during an exercise by a three-ship flight of "723", "734" and "729" in dive bombing and ground target strafing. First Lieutenant Władysław Raczkiewicz did not deploy his airbrakes before the bombing run and set the wrong value of the air pressure on the altimeter. As result, the aircraft attained too high a speed before the bomb release and the bombs were released at an altitude of 1,000 meters, 100 meters lower than required. He did not recover from the dive and was killed.

In 1971 the Słupsk regiment lost MiG-19P "1015". On 22 January, after a high-speed landing approach and touch-down 350 m behind the "T" mark, the brake chute tore off. The fighter overran the runway and the nose wheel strut broke. The starboard wing was torn off after hitting obstacles. The damage was so extensive that the aircraft was scrapped.

Another MiG-19P, "739", was scrapped in 1972. After landing at Słupsk air base the aircraft, flown by Maj. Marian Więciaszek, overran the taxiway and hit obstacles due to brake failure. The aircraft was unrepairable.

On 27 March 1973 the MiG-19P "1023", piloted by Capt. Jan Budek was scrambled to intercept an unidentified aircraft in Polish airspace. Having accomplished the mission the aircraft failed to return to base and went missing. Probably it crashed into the sea, but neither the pilot nor the wreckage were found.

In May 1973 there were 13 MiG-19Ps in the regiment's inventory: "721", "723", "724", "726", "728", "729", "730", "1008", "1011", "1017","1021", "1024" and "1025". In 1974 a decision to retire worn-out MiG-19P and PM fighters was made. The last night flights of the "nineteens", on the last day of their service, 3 December 1974, ended with another mishap. On landing the MiG-19P 1017 the nose landing gear failed to lower, but Maj. Bonifacy Trela completed this flight safely.

29

30

[29]: MiG-19P "1029". The last example of this version delivered to Poland in August 1958. As with most of these aircraft, it was first operated by the Advanced Flying School in Modlin and then transferred to 28. PLM at Słupsk. It was written off after a landing accident on 10 March 1962. The brake chute release mechanism failed and the aircraft, with broken nose-wheel strut, hit a tree beyond the runway.

[30]: 1st Lt Tadeusz Falczyński from 62. PLM at Krzesiny climbs into the cockpit of a MiG-19P.

[31]: MiG-19P "1025", Nowe Miasto air base, 1964.

31

32

*[32]: MiG-19P "724" from the 7th production batch. The aircraft is in natural metal finish, covered with transparent lacquer. When it was assigned to the No. 1 Flight of the 1st Pursuit Squadron (*1 Eskadra Pościgowa*) of 62. PLM, the RP-5 radome was gray. During service in the 39. PLM at Mierzęcice the radomes were repainted dark green. The vertical stabilizer tip was red.*

33

34

[33]: MiG-19P "724" was assigned to No.1 Flight of the Pusuit Squadron of 62. PLM OPL at Krzesiny. The radomes were gray.

[34]: MiG-19P "724" photographed during its service in 39. PLM at Mierzęcice. Both radomes were repainted dark green.

35

[35]: MiG-19P "727" from 39. PLM based at Mierzęcice, delivered to Poland in 1957 in the first batch of these aircraft. The aircraft is in natural metal finish, covered with transparent lacquer. Note the shape and size of the tactical number digits and the tip of the PTB-760 underwing tank, painted white.

36

[36]: MiG-19P "727". This aircraft was lost in a crash on 3 August 1966 in 39. PLM during a night training sortie from the reserve airfield at Kamień Śląski.

37

[37]: MiG-19P "730" from the 7th production batch, assigned to 39. PLM at Mierzęcice in 1964. The aircraft is in natural metal finish, covered with transparent lacquer. The aircraft wears checkerboards with reversed colour pattern. The radomes were dark green. The tips of the vertical stabilizer and under-wing tank were red, as in photo 11.

38

[38]: MiG-19P interceptors at Nowe Miasto air base during assembly before the parade on the 20th anniversary of People's Republic of Poland in 1964. Aircraft "721" is visible in the background, a part of "730" is visible in the foreground. Heat resistant panels are attached to the fuselage sides by the muzzles of the NR-30 cannons. Four gun vents are visible on the wing between the fuselage and the wing fence.

39

[39]: Rear section of "730" with reversed checkerboards. The serial number N620730 is visible on the vertical stabilizer. Cooling air scoops for the RD-9B engine nozzles are visible at the base of the vertical stabilizer. The air scoop on the fuselage at the vertical stabilizer extension provided cooling air for the hydraulic system. MiG-19PM "910" is visible in the background and behind it "724".

40

[40]: MiG-19P "1011" from the 10th production batch, after a brief service in 62. PLM it was transferred to 39. PLM. The aircraft is in natural metal finish, covered with transparent lacquer. The heat resistant panels in front of the cannon muzzles is overpainted. RP-5 radomes remained grey. The vertical stabilizer tip and stabilator anti-flutter mass balances were red.

41

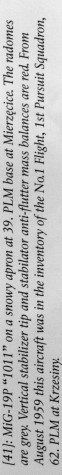

[41]: MiG-19P "1011" on a snowy apron at 39. PLM base at Mierzęcice. The radomes are grey. Vertical stabilizer tip and stabilator anti-flutter mass balances are red. From August 1959 this aircraft was in the inventory of the No.1 Flight, 1st Pursuit Squadron, 62. PLM at Krzesiny.

42

[42]: Capt. Leopold Paul stands next to MiG-19P "1011" operated by 39. PLM. Open brake chute container is visible.

43

[43]: *MiG-19P "1018" from the Air Training Centre* (Centrum Szkolenia Lotniczego) *at Modlin, delivered in the second batch of aircraft from the 10th production batch. The radomes are grey.*

44

[44]: MiG-19P "1018" taxiing after landing during service in the Air Training Centre (CSL) at Modlin, with Capt. Czesław Kantyka at the controls. The radomes are grey.

MiG-19PM

The MiG-19PM was the first interceptor armed with guided air-to-air missiles in the inventory of the Polish air force. In early 1959 twelve MiG-19PM fighters were delivered by rail to Warsaw-Babice airfield. Like the aircraft from the previous two deliveries, they were assembled by factory technicians and flown by the manufacturer's pilots. The aircraft, delivered to the Advanced Pilot School at Modlin and accepted on 20 July 1959, were from the 9th production batch, with serial numbers: 65210902, 65210904, 65210905, 65210906, 65210908, 65210909, 65210910, 65210911, 65210912, 65210914, 65210916 and 65210917. The first two digits of the eight-digit serial number (65) were the product code of the MiG-19PM. The next two digits (21) denoted the production plant (Gorky), then two digits for the number of the production batch and the last two denoted the individual aircraft. Three-digit tactical numbers on the MiG-19PM aircraft were equivalent to the last three digits of the serial number.

This aircraft differed in many ways from the MiG-19P. The armament was the main difference between these two versions operated in Poland, but there were many others.

The MiG-19PM was fitted with RP-2U radar in lieu of the RP-5. The RP-2U radar located the target with greater precision

[45]: MiG-19PM "904" from 28. PLM based at Słupsk towed by a Robur truck.

[46]: MiG-19PM "904" from 28. PLM OPK maintained by ground crews before a parade organized to commemorate Sea and Navy Day in June 1965. This aircraft was lost a year later. During a night sortie on 20 June 1966 the stabilator control system failed and the pilot had to eject. Although the ejection was at an altitude of only about 200 meters, the pilot survived.

47

[47–49]: MiG-19PM "905" at Słupsk air base.

48

49

than the previous one. It featured altered ranges of signalization of the radar's blind zone and safety zone and incorporated a guidance system for RS-2US missiles. These missiles could be launched singly, in pairs or in salvo at certain time intervals. The maximum effective range of the missiles was 3.5 km. The RS-2US missile's weight was 83 kg and speed was 650 m/s. The warhead, with a proximity fuse, weighed 13 kg. The minimum launch distance of the RS-2US missile was 1.5 km. When the missile approached the target, the warhead exploded. The RV-2U Doppler proximity fuse had a target detection range of 15 m. The beam-riding RS-2US missile required constant illumination of the target by the MiG-19PM fighter's radar until hitting the target. It limited the aircraft's maneuvering capability, since it could not make any violent maneuvers until the missile hit the target. Such maneuvers could cause loss of contact with the target and loss of control over the missile. The RS-2US missiles were fitted with a self-destruction system. The effectiveness of the RS-2US missiles carried by the twelve Polish MiG-19PM fighters was (as it is now admitted) limited. The probability of eliminating violently maneuvering targets, such as enemy fighter aircraft, with these missiles was low. Pilots of potential enemy aircraft, who knew the characteristics of the RS-2US missile, would not fly straight and level to allow being shot down. On the other hand the MiG-19PM, armed only with guided air-to-air missiles, after having launched them was defenseless because it had no gun armament. Therefore the sense in purchasing a larger number of cannon-armed MiG-19P fighters rather than missile-only armed PM variants is apparent.

Due to different armament the MiG-19PM had altered cockpit equipment. It was fitted with an S-13-100OS gun camera with longer focal length than the AKS-5 gun camera of the MiG-19S. The MiG-19PM had wings redesigned to be suitable for the new armament. Four underwing pylons for APU-4 rail launchers were installed. Pylons for ORO-57K launchers were removed from the rear of the wings. Since the cannons were removed from the wings, the cannon access panels and gas vents were also removed from the upper surfaces of the wings. The installation of missile launchers under the wings forced relocation of the aileron booster control access hatches to the upper surfaces of the wings.

In the MiG-19PM aircraft purchased by Poland the dorsal fairing, covering bundles of electric and antenna wires and the junction between the fairing and vertical stabilizer base, were identical to equivalent elements on the MiG-19Ps of the 10th production batch (no MiG-19P of the 10th batch survived in Poland, only photographs remain). The MiG-19PM and MiG-19P aircraft of the 10th production batch operated in Poland had identical taller bases of the vertical stabilizer, smooth junctions between the stabilizer base and the dorsal fairing and a similar shape to the kerosene and gasoline fillers inspection hatch, located on the starboard side of the upper fuselage, aft of the sliding canopy fairing.

The MiG-19PM differed from the MiG-19P variant in having a rudder trim tab, actuated by a UT-6 electric actuator. Thus on the starboard side of the rudder there was a small access hatch for the electric actuator, and oval bulges, housing the UT-6 actuator, were placed on both sides of the rudder.

[50]: MiG-19PM "905" at Słupsk air base. UIł-28 "S5" is visible in the background.

51

[51]: MiG-19PM "905" at Słupsk air base, in a portrait photograph by Zbigniew Chmurzyński. Underwing tanks are marked with the aircraft number "905".

The vertical stabilizer of the MiG-19PM differed in some details from that of the MiG-19P version. On both sides of the stabilizer flat ORD-2 antennas of the SOD 57M transponder, enabling individual aircraft identification, were installed. The MiG-19P had no ORD-2 antenna on the vertical stabilizer, only a hatch was situated in that place on the port side. A detachable panel for access to antenna wire connections and electric wires, supplying power to the antennas and position light on the stabilizer, was located on the stabilizer's leading edge. The access hatch for engine exhaust nozzle control valves on the starboard side of the stabilizer was larger and mounted horizontally. In the MiG-19P this hatch was smaller and placed at an angle to the fuselage.

The take-off weight of the MiG-19PM was 300 kg heavier than the P variant. This factor, combined with higher aerodynamic drag induced by four underwing pylons with APU-4 rail launchers, meant that the performance of the MiG-19PM was poorer. In clean configuration – without underwing tanks and missiles – it attained a speed of 1,250 km/h at 11,000 m. In Poland, flights at supersonic speeds by the MiG-19PM with underwing tanks and missiles were not made.

The pilots flying the MiG-19PMs were trained in the USSR in intercepting and engaging aerial targets with RS-2US missiles. The first group of pilots departed in early 1958 by train for Moscow, from where they travelled on a Li-2 aircraft to Savasleyka airfield. Here they underwent theoretical training during April and May. Next the Polish pilots had to make train-

52

53

[52]: A visit by party and government officials to the 28. PLM at Słupsk. On this occasion RS-2US were mounted on MiG-19PM "905".

[53]: Underwing pylons with APU-4 ejector racks for RS-2US guided missiles, on MiG-19PM "905".

ing flights, assessing their flying technique. This recurring stage of training was redundant for them, since all were First Class-rated pilots. The organizers wanted to impose a higher cost training. The main part of the combat training was commenced in early June 1958 at Krasnovodsk air base in Turkmenistan, near the Caspian Sea coast. The missile range, suited for live fire exercises with air-to-air guided missiles, was located in the nearby Kara-Kum desert. The three week training in use of RS-2US missiles consisted of a week of theoretical training and two weeks of practical exercises, comprising several training flights, followed by launching a salvo of two live missiles. They were fired at Lavochkin La-17 target drones, launched by Tu-4 bombers – unlicensed copies of the Boeing B-29 (according to Soviet terminology the Tu-4 was not a copy, but an analogue). The base of the Tu-4 mother ships was located near Bekdash on a peninsula closing Kara Bogaz bay. The Tu-4 with two La-17 drones under the wings reached an altitude of 7,000–8,000 meters after about two hours and launched the drones at this altitude.

The hosts provided their own MiG-19PMs with ground crews for the training. The training comprised introduction to navigation over desert areas, rescue procedures and alternate airfields. The program of this stage of training comprised familiarization flights on a MiG-19PM without external stores and then with two RS-2US missiles to make the pilot acquainted with the altered aerodynamic characteristics of the aircraft. After the completion of all necessary training and exercises in the first half of June, live missile launch sorties against target drones over Kara-Kum desert began. The fighters took off in pairs to intercept the Tu-4 bomber with two La-17 drones prepared for drop launch. Each pilot launched two missiles in salvo at the drone already aloft (first the leader and then the wingman). The first live fire exercise with RS-2US missiles was completed as planned, but one pair of pilots experienced a dramatic situation when launching missiles at the target drone. The leading pilot had to abort the attack due to malfunction of the RP-2U radar. The wingman found himself in much worse situation. After the trigger was unlocked two RS-2US missiles were launched one after another and the guidance beam of the RP-2U radar shifted to the Tu-4 aircraft and both missiles rode the beam. He brought the situation under control, switching the radar to "locked beam" mode and banked to the left, and the two missiles, still riding the beam, repeated this maneuver. Several seconds later both missiles self-destructed and the Tu-4 returned to Bekdash base. The pilot who encountered this dramatic situation was 1st Lt Edward Sztandera. Later it was revealed that the trouble was caused by malfunction of the radar switch, but the local counter-intelligence officer initially suggested this was a deliberate attempt by the Polish pilot to shoot down the Tu-4 and escape to nearby Iran... Finally the pilot was acquitted of all charges and could continue training.

During the next live fire exercises in the USSR the unreliability of RP-2U radar was still a major problem. However, some changes were made in the program of the training courses, an example of which is the training of MiG-19P and PM pilots from 28. PLM and 39. PLM in 1962. This time a group of Polish officers departed Warsaw aboard two Il-14 aircraft, taking RS-2US missiles in crates with them. The route ran via Lvov, where a Soviet navigator and wireless operator joined them. After the theoretical training, before the first sorties Polish trainees were taken for a flight around the exercise area aboard an An-2 fitted with an additional fuel tank. During this flight possible alternate airfields, including Ashgabat, were visited (only from the air, without landing), their location revealed in

54

[54]: MiG-19PMs which survived until the end of service in 28. PLM: "905" in the foreground and "911" and "916" by the fence.

[55–56]: Officers of the Polish Navy in 28. PLM at Słupsk standing beside MiG-19PM "908". Note the tactical number with characteristic shape of the digit "8". The digits were painted with a stencil with large gaps, not painted over.

[57]: Aircraft "909" with a towbar attached to the nosewheel.

[58]: Ground crews working on MiG-19PM "909" on the flightline at Słupsk air base. The aircraft is still partially covered with tarpaulins. Note the characteristic canopy cover.

59

[59]: *Take-off of a pair of 39. PLM fighters from Mierzęcice air base. The lead aircraft is MiG-19PM "912".*

60

[60]: *A part of the tail section of MiG-19PM "912" with incorrect colour pattern of the checkerboard, lacking white. A static discharger is visible on the wingtip. Characteristic features of the PM version are a removable antenna and electric wire access panel on the leading edge of the vertical stabilizer, rudder trim tab and ORD-2 IFF antenna visible below the stabilizer tip.*

[61]: *Flightline of 28. PLM OPK aircraft at Słupsk air base. MiG-19PM "912" is visible in the foreground. Standing behind it are MiG-19Ps "724" and "1024".*

61

case of possible emergency landings. The first sorties were made without the missiles, then with two missiles without launching them. Taking their own RS-2US missiles from Poland to the USSR enabled the pilots to train in subsequent sorties the necessary maneuvers related to guiding missiles to the target. Poland had no proper firing range for this kind of exercise, where the pilot could track the missile's flight after the launch, when the missile initially descended and then climbed and, after having covered a specific distance, was destroyed by the self-destruction system. As aerial targets, decommissioned and converted MiG-15bis were used. The use of Tu-4 bombers as mother ships for target drones was abandoned.

The MiG-19PM's engine was started by a mechanic on the runway. Having engaged the autopilot the mechanic disembarked and closed the cockpit. The aircraft took off on a radio command from the ground and in the air it was guided by a Yak-25 two-seat aircraft. However, the Polish pilots did not practice realistic situations, because the MiG-15 target drone made no evasive maneuvers, to help make shooting it down more difficult. Furthermore, the Polish pilots flew without underwing tanks, and after the attack they were warned by Yak-25 crews about a possible lack of fuel, preventing a return to base. During the training the leaders of three pairs had trouble with unreliable guidance radars.

In July 1959 five MiG-19PM aircraft, "902", "904", "905", "906" and "908", were transferred from Modlin to the Słupsk regiment. The regiment based at Mierzęcice received the following MiG-19PMs: "910", "911", "912", "914" and "917".

In the late 1960s an idea was conceived to use MiG-19PM interceptors for attacking ground targets with RS-2US guided

[63]: Pinholes on the surface of the dielectric radome of radar searching antenna of "914", visible in the light at night. Note two different flight suits of 28. PLM pilots.

62

63

64

[62+64]: Two night photographs of MiG-19PM "914". RS-2US missiles mounted on underwing pylons are covered with tarpaulins.

65 *[65]: MiG-19PM "914" decelerating after touchdown. Brake chute, wing flaps, ventral and side airbrakes are deployed.*

66 *[66]: MiG-19PM "914" (serial number visible on the vertical stabilizer) and MiG-19P "1012" during assembly at Nowe Miasto air base in 1964.*

67

[67]: 760-liter PTB-760 underwing fuel tank. Pylon and struts attaching it to the wing are visible. The checkerboard on the lower surface of the wing of "914" is nearly completely peeled off, only the outline is visible. Serial number 650914 is visible under the rear section of the wing root.

missiles and ARS-212M and ARS-60 unguided rockets. The objective was to support ground forces, which were to implement the insane Soviet doctrine of an assault on Western Europe. Adding a Polish air component with Su-7 aircraft conducting nuclear strikes, the effect of these Soviet-planned operations would have been a radioactive wasteland in place of the former People's Republic of Poland after retaliatory strikes.

In 1961 two MiG-19PM aircraft were lost in the 28. PLM. 906 was written off after a failure caused by pilot error on 13 September. Sadly, two days later "902" was lost in a crash during a night flight, probably due to failure of the stabilator automatic control system (ARU-2V). Second Lieutenant Jan Drewicz was killed.

On landing at Słupsk air base the brake chute was ripped apart and the nosewheel tyre blew up in MiG-19PM "908" from 28. PLM. The aircraft overran the runway and was rolling on the grass when the nosewheel collapsed and the aircraft's nose section was damaged. The aircraft was repaired and returned to service.

During 11–15 November 1965 pilots of 39. PLM at Mierzęcice ferried the following MiG-19PM aircraft to Słupsk: "910", "911", "912", "914" and "917". From that month on there were no PM variants at Mierzęcice, all were gathered in the 28. PLM at Słupsk.

In 1966 two MiG-19PM fighters were lost in the 28. PLM. Fortunately, in both cases the pilots survived. On 20 June due to another failure of the ARU-2V system in "904" during a night flight, the pilot had to eject. The ejection was successful despite the low altitude (about 200 meters) and the pilot was unhurt. A month later during MiG-19PM type

68

[68]: A MiG-19PM covered with tarpaulins, with only a fragment of the digit "6" visible (probably "916"). The forward tarpaulin is marked with the number "905".

[69]: Bulbous fairing enlarging the capacity of the main wheel well, with short wing fence riveted to it.

conversion a pilot erroneously switched the landing gear lever before commencing the take-off roll. The landing gear retracted during the take-off roll and the aircraft collapsed on the runway, skidding on the forward fuselage and underwing tanks until it stopped. The pilot managed to escape from the aircraft, which caught fire and burned.

From the latter half of the 1960s the failure rate of the "nineteens", with which the ground crews had to deal, was significantly increasing. Shortage of spare parts grounded a large number of aircraft. Engine failures were frequent. Despite the fact that the aircraft were powered by two engines, there was no guarantee of safety when one engine quit in flight. Failures of the ARU-2V automatic stabilator control system were commonplace.

69

[70]: Take-off of a pair of interceptors from Mierzęcice air base. The lead aircraft retracting its landing gear is MiG-19PM "917".

70

Up to May 1973 the following MiG-19PM aircraft remained in service: "905", "908", "909", "911", "912", "914", "916" and "917".

In May 1973 there were in total 21 MiG-19P and MiG-19PM aircraft in the inventory of the 28. PLM at Słupsk. When the regiment received MiG-21MF fighters, it underwent structural changes in accordance with the new complement No. 20/115. Within the regiment were two squadrons of 18 aircraft each: 1st Squadron, equipped with MiG-19P and PM fighters (CO: Maj. Alojzy Zgondek) and 2nd Squadron with MiG-21MF fighters (CO: Maj. Ignacy Jonik). In 1974 the 1st Squadron was plagued by numerous malfunctions and there were three serious failures of the "nineteens": "1024", "905" and "1017". The MiG-19P "1024" flown by Lt Col. Tadeusz Gut had an engine failure, but the pilot managed to make an emergency landing at the base. Next was the landing gear failure of MiG-19PM "905". By 3 December, at the end of 15 years of service, 18 aircraft survived (only 10 of them airworthy), half of the total number of 36 fighters purchased. The end of service of the first supersonic fighters in Poland was received in the Słupsk regiment without regret. As an unwritten story says, one of the officers

71

[71]: Open ground power socket panel of "917". A belt securing the canopy to the wing trailing edge is visible.

[72]: Ground crews servicing RP-2U radar electronic blocks raised from the electronic gear compartment.

72

73

74

[73]: MiG-19PM "917" seen from below. The port aileron is fitted with a trim tab. The checkerboard is painted without white squares, not exactly in parallel with the wing sweep angle. Main wheel well door with hydraulic strut is visible.

[74]: Crew chief of "917" disconnects the ground power cable from the socket. Port airbrake is visible next to the checkerboard.

[75]: MiG-19PM "917" ready to take-off.

75

[76]: Capt. Władysław Waltoś in partial pressure suit in front of MiG-19PM "917". Serial number N650917 is visible. EKSR-46 signal flare dispenser is visible in the vertical stabilizer base.

76

[77]: A pilot with seat pack parachute climbs the ladder to the cockpit of MiG-19PM "917". Ventral airbrake lowered at low angle is visible. The taxiing light visible on the port side aft of the nosewheel well illuminated the area in front and left of the aircraft (10 degrees).

77

78

[78–79]: TP-19 brake chute, 15 sq.m in area. The canopy has the shape of decagon inscribed in a circle 4.497 m in diameter.

79

[80]: RS-2US air-to-air guided missiles on APU-4 launcher racks of mounted under the wing of a MiG-19PM fighter.

[81]: A motley of aircraft types in front of the hangar at Modlin. Standing farthest away are two "19s" of the ATC, and Il-28 86 from 35. PLB is visible in the foreground.

kissed the concrete of the airfield with relief. The remaining "nineteens" that had survived until retirement were preserved in 1975 and gathered in a hangar. The aircraft 736 and 1018 served as technical aids in Air Force Technical Officer School in Oleśnica. 905 and 728 were donated to museums in Cracow and Kołobrzeg. 908 was placed as a monument at Słupsk air base. A MiG-19P stood as a monument in front of the railway station in Świdwin until the 1980s. When the write-off documents were accepted by Air Force Headquarters in February 1976, engines were removed from some aircraft and sent to the USSR, where they were used as powerplants for Lavochkin La-17 target drones. Airframes without engines were intended for gunnery range targets and were transferred to Nadarzyce gunnery and bombing range in 1976.

This is the opinion of Gen. Jerzy Gotowała PhD about the MiG-19: "*It was not the best and safest design. The aircraft had wings swept at high angle, two quite powerful, but unreliable turbojet engines with afterburner and sophisticated avionics, which absorbed most of pilot's attention. The all-weather interceptor could be flown only by experienced high-time pilots. There is no wonder that the introduction of the MiG-19 caused deterioration of flying safety*".

82

[82]: "Arrowhead" formation consisting of 16 MiG-19P and MiG-19PM fighters during the parade on 22 July 1966. This formation was led by Maj. Franciszek Koźlak from 28. PLM.

83

[83]: Port side of a MiG-19P from the second delivery (10th production batch).

[84]: „905" preserved at Polish Aviation Museum in Cracow. The tall (32 cm) wing fence has three vertical cuts preventing the fence from cracking when the wing deforms in flight. The dorsal fairing housing antenna and electric wires is, in the PM version, wider and taller than in P versions of the 7th production batch. The junction with the vertical stabilizer base is smooth.

[85]: Capt. Czesław Ciapała from 39. PLM based at Mierzęcice next to a MiG-19P from the second delivery (10th production batch). The dorsal fairing is of the same height and width as in the PM variant. As in the PM version the junction between the vertical stabilizer base and fairing is smooth, without a sharp angle.

[86]: MiG-19P from the first delivery (7th production batch) preserved at Kołobrzeg museum in 1978 with false "723" number rather than correct "728". The junction of the vertical stabilizer base with short, narrow dorsal fairing is at an angle.

[87]: MiG-19PM "908" preserved at the former base of the disbanded 28. PLM at Słupsk, photographed by Wacław Hołyś.

88

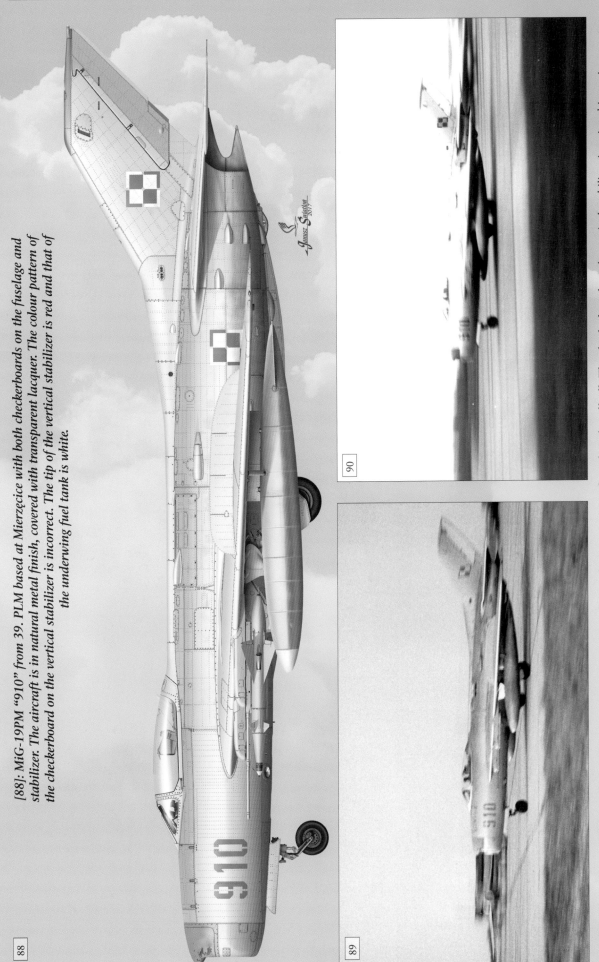

[88]: *MiG-19PM "910" from 39. PLM based at Mierzęcice with both checkerboards on the fuselage and stabilizer. The aircraft is in natural metal finish, covered with transparent lacquer. The colour pattern of the checkerboard on the vertical stabilizer is incorrect. The tip of the vertical stabilizer is red and that of the underwing fuel tank is white.*

89

90

[89–90]: *Two photos of MiG-19PM "910" taken by Janusz Szymański, emphasizing its speed on the take-off roll. The checkerboard on the vertical stabilizer is painted in an incorrect colour pattern and on the fuselage is correct. This aircraft was lost on 20 July 1966. The nosewheel retracted on take-off, the aircraft still rolled on the main wheels, grinding the forward fuselage section against concrete until it stop. The pilot escaped. Fuel leaking from damaged tanks caught fire and the aircraft burnt out.*

91

[91]: MiG-19PM “916” from 28. PLM based at Słupsk. The aircraft is in natural metal finish, covered with transparent lacquer. No fuselage checkerboard. RP-2U radome is green.

92

[92]: MiG-19PM “916”, large checkerboard on the vertical stabilizer. The MiG-19P “1021” is visible in the background.

93

[93]: MiG-19PM "917" from 39. PLM, wearing two checkerboards of various sizes. The checkerboard on the vertical stabilizer has no white squares and outlines. The aircraft is in natural metal finish, covered with transparent lacquer. The radome is green and the vertical stabilizer tip is red. Top of right underwing fuel tank is red.

94

[94]: MiG-19PM "917" connected to a ground power unit mounted on a ZiL-164 truck.

95

[95]: MiG-19PM "917" from 39. PLM, being prepared for take-off at Mierzęcice air base. Note the checkerboard on the fuselage with paint peeling off. It is much smaller than that on the vertical stabilizer, which has no white squares painted.

MiG-21F-13

The MiG-21F-13 was the first fighter aircraft in Poland capable of exceeding twice the speed of sound. It was a single engine aircraft, built in the USSR as a lightweight fighter for daylight clear weather operations. The introduction of the MiG-21 to the inventory of the Polish air force was named "the second technological revolution" and the fighters themselves were initially nicknamed "deltas" and then "fast movers".

Poland, as a politically disloyal ally of the USSR after 1956, did not receive clearance for series production of these advanced Mach 2+ fighters because the USSR did not trust the new Polish party authorities. Czechoslovakia, giving no reasons for distrust, received clearance and licence documentation for production of the next type of supersonic fighter (after the MiG-19S). There was no MiG-21 production in Poland, although the designation Lim-7 was earmarked for them. Only the possibility of purchase remained, although even this way of acquisition of the aircraft by costly import was not easy. The Soviet side was reluctant to sell the new fighters. The reason was the refusal to purchase the worthless two-seat Yak-27R reconnaissance aircraft by the Polish side. The sale of 24–30 such aircraft was strongly urged by the Soviets during 1962–1963. The Polish air force owed the rejection of this offer to the resolute attitude of the CO of the Air and Aerial Defense Forces, Brig. Gen Jan Frey-Bielecki.

The MiG-21F-13 was a mid-wing aircraft with delta wing with clipped tips and all-flying tail. Some experience gained during design of the MiG-19 aircraft was used, but its concept

96

[96]: The first MiG-21F-13 delivered to Modlin. The aircraft features a supersonic air intake with movable inlet cone, adjusting the area of the intake depending on the speed. 30 mm cannon muzzle and behind it a deflected airbrake are visible on the starborad side of the aircraft. Sitting in the cockpit is Maj. Kazimierz Kamiński.

[97]: Automatic bleed air doors are located on the sides of the forward fuselage and above the cannon an auxiliary take-off air intake, protected with a grid cover, is visible.

[98]: Brig. Gen Jan Raczkowski poses in front of MiG-21F-13 "1217" at Modlin airfield.

[99]: MiG-21F-13 "1217" on the flightline at Modlin airfield.

[100–101]: MiG-21F-13 "1217" from ATC Modlin, with the tactical number changed on the occasion of New Year 1967. On the air data probe the aircraft's tactical number "1217" is visible. This aircraft was operated only by ATC Modlin and did not serve in any combat unit. In the 1990s it was sold to a private collection in Hermeskeil, Germany, where it has been put on display without Polish markings.

[102–103]: MiG-21F-13 "2008" at Bydgoszcz airfield during the I Central Aerial Reconnaissance Competition of the Armed Forces of the People's Republic of Poland in 1971.

[104]: MiG-21F-13 "2008" assigned to 2. PLM at Goleniów during a night flight.

[105]: MiG-21F-13 "2008" assigned to 2. PLM at Goleniów with a towbar attached to the nosewheel.

was not suitable for a Mach 2+ aircraft. The powerplant of the MiG-19, comprising two engines, resulted in high demand for fuel and operating fluids and increased the aircraft's weight. The design of RD-9 engine was at the peak of its development and did not offer the possibility of delivering high thrust in the future. Likewise, swept wings with high aspect ratio did not provide the necessary stiffness at high speeds and produced high drag. Thus the new fast fighter aircraft featured a delta wing, but not in "clean" form but with conventional empennage, and a single R-11F-300 engine ("F" stood for engine with afterburner, "300" was the code number of Tumanski engine plant). This was an advanced two-spool axial-flow turbojet engine with two separate, independent compressors – low and high pressure turbines of coaxial rotation. The aircraft featured a streamlined fuselage of elliptical cross-section, designed in accordance with the area rule. The supersonic central air intake was fitted with a movable inlet cone, which automatically adjusted the area of the intake depending on the airspeed. Up to a speed of Ma=1.5 the cone was retracted. Between the speeds of Ma=1.5 – Ma=1.9 the cone deployed to the middle position and was deployed fully forward when the aircraft exceeded a speed of Ma=1.9. On both sides of the streamlined fuselage, automatically controlled bleed air doors were placed, which together with the movable inlet cone reduced thrust losses at supersonic speeds. Below the cockpit additional (take-off) air intakes were placed, which, when open, provided extra air for the engine on the ground and during take-off. A characteristic feature of the MiG-21F-13 was the PVD-5 air data probe on a boom mounted below the air intake, which was raised as in the MiG-19S when the aircraft was on the ground.

The one-piece canopy hinged forward. The MiG-21F-13 was fitted with the SK-1 egress system, which enabled the pilot to bail out at speeds up to 1,100 km/h. The minimum ejection altitude was 110 m. During ejection at speeds exceeding 750 km/h the canopy was not jettisoned (so as not to disturb the ejection) as in earlier fighters. It was taken with the pilot, staying with the seat and protecting the pilot against the slipstream. A 62 mm thick bulletproof glass section was mounted inside the cockpit, under the jettisonable canopy. The pilots were equipped with VKK-4 partial pressure suits. Beneath the fuselage, between the wheel wells, a 490-liter external tank was carried. Two airbrakes were mounted to the 11th former on both sides of the fuselage and ae third, downward–opening, airbrake was mounted on the 13th former. On the lower aft fuselage a 35.2 cm tall ventral fin was mounted. The forward section of this housed the antenna of the Lazur telemetry system, under a dielectric fairing. The brake chute, 16 m^2 in area, was housed in a bay on the port side of the ventral fin, as in the MiG-19. The delta wing, swept at 57°, had a 2° anhedral. On the upper surfaces of the wings small wing fences, improving aileron effectiveness, were mounted.

In contrast to the MiG-19, the MiG-21F-13 had no search radar. This shortcoming meant that this first version of the MiG-21 was deemed unpromising and "blind" after the

106

[106]: Seven MiG-21F-13 fighters on the flightline at Goleniów airfield. The first three aircraft are "2009", "2007" and "2018".

[107]: The aircraft "2008" and "2009" from 2. PLM at Goleniów. Along with "2007" they were transferred to this unit from ATC Modlin in July 1967.

107

108

[108]: Winter scenery at Goleniów airfield with MiG-21F-13 fighters "802", "2009" and "2224" serving as reserve aircraft. Visible behind them are MiG-21PFMs "4911" and "5002", delivered to Poland on 23 January 1967.

109

[109–110]: MiG-21F-13 "2016" being prepared for a sortie at Krzesiny air base in November 1962.

110

111

[111]: MiG-21F-13 "2016" in the hangar of 62. PLM at Krzesiny air base. PVD-5 air data probe with electrically-heated pitch and yaw vanes are mounted on elevated boom. In flight they aligned with the airstream. This aircraft was lost in a crash on 20 November 1963.

112

[112]: The aircraft "2018" from 62. PLM OPK, damaged on 16 January 1964. The aircraft made an emergency landing with the engine on fire. Since the manufacturer acknowledged the failure as a manufacturing defect, the repair was made in the USSR and the aircraft returned to service.

113

[113–114]: MiG-21F-13 "2018" from 2. PLM "Kraków" at Bydgoszcz airfield. Along with "2008" it took part in the I Central Aerial Reconnaissance Competition in 1971.

114

[115]: MiG-21F-13 "2018" among MiG-21PFM fighters at Goleniów airfield. The different forward fuselage sections of these two versions are visible.

introduction of MiG-21PF and PFM variants with RM-21 Sapfir radar. In the MiG-21F-13 the ASP-5ND gunsight, coupled with SRD-5M ranging radar, was used for aiming. The R-3S (K-13) air-to-air missile, carried on APU-13 underwing launchers and fitted with an infra-red seeker head, was an unlicensed copy of the US AIM-9B Sidewinder missile. The Soviets captured several Sidewinder missiles where they failed to explode after launch. On 28 November 1958 the Council of Ministers decided to reverse-engineer it. In the USSR copying foreign designs was "customarily" not admitted, claiming that this was "not a copy, but an analogue". However, the reverse-engineered missiles were no match for the US originals. The designers of the MiG-21F-13 decided that there was no need to equip it with radar. It resulted from the opinion that that the new passive heat-seeking missiles were such perfect weapon that after launch they would follow the target on their own. Launched missiles did not always fly to the target. The disadvantage of this missile was its vulnerability to weather conditions and thermal decoys. The missile's seeker did not distinguish the real target from a false one – a thermal decoy. The R-3S missile could not engage targets maneuvering with g-loads in excess of 2. The attacking target had chances of survival by making a sharp turn towards the missile or making an "escape into the sun". Alternatively, on two underwing pylons two UB-16-57U launchers with 16 S-5 57 unguided rockets each, two S-24 240 mm unguided missiles or two bombs weighing up to 500 kg, could be carried to attack ground targets. The gun armament consisted of one NR-30 cannon with 60 rounds, mounted on the port side of the fuselage below the cockpit.

On 29 June 1961 a Soviet pilot ferried the first MiG-21F-13, serial number 741217, from the Soviet 582nd Fighter Regiment, based at Chojna. This aircraft landed without fanfare, with no national insignia or tactical number, at Modlin airfield. The personnel of the Air Training Centre was not trained to maintain it yet. It was stored and guarded by armed sentinels in the hangar of the 1st Air Squadron of the ATC, just emptied out of MiG-19 aircraft previously stored there. The aircraft required routine flights to maintain airworthiness. Therefore a pilot and mechanic came by air to Modlin from the Soviet regiment at Chojna. The MiG-21entered the inventory of ATC Modlin on 22 September 1961, with tactical number "1217" (the last four digits of the serial number).

In late September 1961 sixteen Polish pilots were sent to the air and technical training centre in Krasnodar for conversion to the new type. In the flying group there were eight pilots from the 1st Squadron of 62. PLM OPK based at Krzesiny, which was to be the first operational unit to re-equip with the MiG-21F-13. Apart from pilots, a large group of maintenance personnel was undergoing training at a separate course in Krasnodar. The Soviet side planned the duration of the training course of Polish pilots to last for several months, but it was apparent that it would be protracted. Extended ground preparatory courses and series of lectures by the Soviet instructors took many weeks. The Krasnodar training centre had no two-seat trainer version at that time (the first prototype of the MiG-21U flew only on 17 October 1960 and the initial three production MiG-21U (Type 66, *izdeliye* 66-400) combat trainers were built in No. 31 plant in Tbilisi in 1962). Until December 1961 the pilots in training spent only 3 hours each at the controls

116

[116]: MiG-21F-13 pilots in VKK-4 partial pressure suits with two helmet types. The aircraft "2018" is visible in the background.

117

118

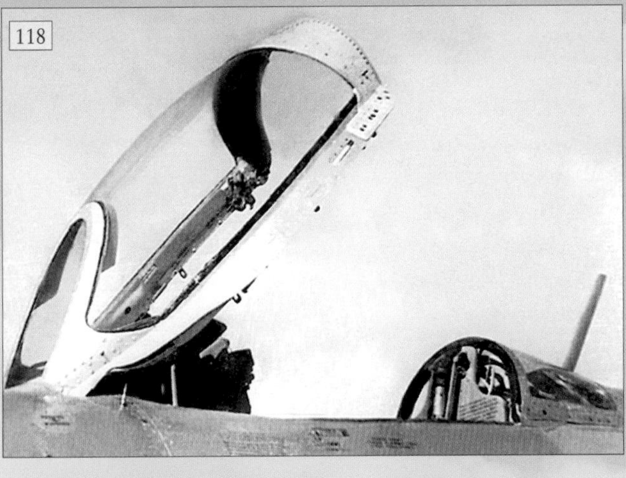

[117]: Forward-hinged jettisonable canopy. 62 mm thick armored glass is visible inside the cockpit.

[118]: Open cockpit of MiG-21F-13. SK-1 ejection seat is removed.

119

[119]: Maj. K. Krata wearing the closed-type flight helmet, which after being sealed with the glass cover he is holding served also as an oxygen mask. Brake chute line attachment hook is located in the ventral fin extension.

120

[120]: Major K. Krata in the cockpit. The helmet is sealed and connected to the radio and oxygen system.

121

122

[121]: MiG-21F-13 "2220" in the hangar of 62. PLM at Krzesiny air base. This aircraft was written off after being damaged by the pilot of "2016", who caused a mid-air collision, leading to the crash of his aircraft in which he was killed.

[122+124–125]: Refueling of "2220" from a Skoda Avia 706R bowser.
[123]: Maj. Kazimierz Krata in front of "2220". PVD-5 air data probe is raised for maintenance.

123

124

125

of the new fighter. Poor organization of the training, as well as an unpleasant atmosphere and disagreements, starting in Krasnodar when a precious aircraft with a Polish pilot overran the runway and was damaged, caused premature termination of the training course and the return of Polish pilots to the homeland in December 1961. A group of four instructor pilots from ATC Modlin, Maj. Kazimierz Kamiński, Capt. Stanisław Radziejowski, 1st Lt Wiesław Komuda and 1st Lt Stanisław Chreptowicz, was sent to the Soviet 582nd Fighter Regiment based at Chojna in Poland to complete the training course. This regiment was already equipped with MiG-21F and F13 fighters.

After the training in Poland the four pilots began flying at ATC Modlin in July 1962. Preparations for training more pilots on the new fighters were ongoing. After completion of the training of the first Polish instructors in the USSR and Chojna, and completion of the training centre, the training of Polish pilots in Modlin began in earnest in the summer of 1962. The aircraft number "1217", operated by the ATC for more than a year, was joined by five factory-fresh aircraft, with serial numbers 742007, 742008, 742009, 742016 and 742017, on 19 September 1962. A further three aircraft, 742015, 742018 and 742019, were delivered two days later, on 21 September. Henceforth there were nine MiG-21F-13 aircraft in the inventory of the 1st Air Squadron of the ATC. Four aircraft, 742015, 742016, 742017 and 742018, were intended for transfer to the 62. PLM OPK based at Krzesiny, but were first used during the first training course conducted at the ATC in October. The pilots of 62. PLM OPK, who had not completed training in Krasnodar, finished training at Modlin. In Modlin, as in Krasnodar, there was no two-seat trainer version yet. The first MiG-21U (66-400), serial number 661220, entered the ATC inventory as late as 18 May 1965. Until that moment the pilots converted to the new Mach 2 fighter directly from Lim-5 and MiG-19P/PM fighters.

The first operational unit in Poland equipped with MiG-21F-13 fighters was 62. PLM OPK based at Krzesiny (3rd Aerial Defence Corps). On 22 October 1962 four aircraft were taken over from ATC Modlin, 742015, 742016, 742017 and 742018. The first sorties on the new fighters were flown from Krzesiny air base on 6 November 1962. Another batch of four aircraft was delivered from the USSR on 11 January 1963. These were serial numbers 742220, 742223, 742224 and 742307. In 1963 a further two fighter regiments, based at Mińsk Mazowiecki and Debrzno, received factory-fresh MiG-21F-13s from the USSR, six each. The introduction of advanced MiG-21F-13 fighters was a breakthrough for these units, previously operating subsonic Lim-5 and Lim-5P fighters. The significance of this event resembled the conversion from piston to jet-powered fighters ten years earlier. Aircraft with serial numbers 740802, 740803, 740804, 740805, 740806 and 740807 were delivered to the 1. PLM OPK (1st Aerial Defence Corps) at Mińsk Mazowiecki on 14 September 1963. They landed at Janów airfield. On 16 September aircraft with numbers 740808, 740809, 740811,740812, 740813 and 740814 were delivered to the 11. PLM based at Debrzno (2nd Aerial Defence Corps). Aircraft from the 8th production batch received tactical numbers comprising the last three digits of the serial number. These were the last MiG-21F-13 aircraft delivered to Poland. Henceforth, each of the three Aerial Defence Corps had Mach 2 fighters, capable of more efficient service in the national air defence system. Introduction of modern interceptors also required more advanced exercises in firing R-3S guided missiles. Live fire exercises with these missiles were conducted in the USSR at the Astrakhan missile range. The first such exercise, in which pilots from ATC Modlin and 62 PLM.OPK took part, were conducted in August 1963.

In 1963 a display team in three MiG-21F-13 aircraft was formed in the 62. PLM OPK from the initiative of Col. Władysław Hermaszewski. The task of forming the team was entrusted to Capt. Jerzy Makarewicz, the CO of the 1st Squadron. He also became the team leader. The right wingman was 1st Lt Tadeusz Falczyński and the left wingman was 1st Lt Wawrzyniec Czapiga. The display program was developed and, after receiving acceptance, the team commenced flight training in the spring of 1963.

The display program comprised arrival at 950 km/h and an altitude of 100–150 meters, a loop, a hammerhead and again a loop. This sequence was repeated twice or thrice, depending on the time limit. Having executed the last loop, the aircraft branched off in the so-called tulip maneuver. During preparations for the program Capt. Makarewicz flew first as the left and then the right wingman. The first display was flown by the team on 9 July 1963 over Krzesiny air base, during a visit by the Hungarian defence minister. Another aerobatic display was flown by the pilots from Krzesiny at the base of

126

127

[126–127]: Front and rear photos of "2220" taken by Janusz Szymański from a "frog" perspective emphasize beautiful, intriguing silhouette of this advanced delta-winged fighter in Polish service.

the 1. PLM "Warsaw" at Mińsk Mazowiecki. Apart from the Polish generals, the spectators were the Soviet Marshal Rodion Malinovsky and representatives of the USSR's Ministry of Defence. Maj. Kazimierz Krata performed a solo flight display in a MiG-21F-13 and then his colleagues of the Krzesiny display team – Capt. Makarewicz and Lieutenants Falczyński and Czapiga – flew their performance. After the display the marshal, reluctant to praise anybody, congratulated the Poles on mastering flying the type in such a short time. Not only was the display itself sensational, but also the fact that apart from the Poles nobody flew aerobatics, let alone team aerobatics, on MiG-21F-13 supersonic fighters.

On 20 November 1963 in the 62. PLM OPK a fatal crash took place during an aerial target interception training sortie. The aircraft acting as aerial target was MiG-21F-13 "2220" flying at an altitude of 10,000 m and speed of 900 km/h, piloted by Maj. Ludwik Podraza. First Lieutenant Wawrzyniec Czapiga took off in MiG-21F-13 2016 and intercepted the target and then, having completed the exercise, both fighters headed for base. The aircraft flown by 1st Lt Czapiga, illicitly approaching to a formation landing collided with Maj. Podraza's aircraft. Lt Czapiga was killed and his airplane crashed on the airfield. Maj. Podraza managed to land his damaged aircraft safely. His airplane was written off due to extensive damage.

128

[128]: Pilot in closed cockpit. Armored glass is visible under the canopy. Note the edges of the panels of the wing skin.

129

[129]: Clearly visible design details of the aircraft: extended port airbrake, main landing gear, ventral tank pylon and landing light.

Luckily there was no loss of a third MiG-21F-13 "2018" in the 62. PLM OPK on 16 January 1964. After a night cross-country sortie and with the circuit to land completed, the aircraft had an engine malfunction and fire on the final approach. The fighter lost the main landing gear wheels, then the nosewheel and the ventral tank on touchdown. The manufacturer admitted a manufacturing defect of the engine and the aircraft underwent overhaul in the USSR during 1966–67. It returned to service, but was assigned to the 2. PLM "Kraków" based at Goleniów (renamed from 4. PLM LO on 4 May 1967).

In the 11. PLM OPK at Debrzno, near the end of MiG-21F-13 service in this unit, the aircraft 811 was damaged. During landing at Debrzno air base on 18 June 1964 the right main wheel tyre was destroyed and the fragments of the blown-up tyre damaged the wing undersurface. The aircraft was grounded until the repair was completed. Due to the repair it remained with the unit until March of the next year, although the remaining examples of this variant were withdrawn from service in August 1964.

In 1964 the regiments based at Krzesiny, Mińsk Mazowiecki and Debrzno began receiving more advanced MiG-21PF aircraft. Although having only a few design changes, these aircraft outclassed the previous version without radar (thus called "blind"). They were equipped with RP-21 radar and "Lazur" datalink for cooperation with the "Vozdukh-1P" automatic ground-controlled intercept (GCI) system. Thus in August that year the aforementioned regiments ceased operations on MiG-21F-13 fighters and began transferring them to other units. They were distributed between the 13. PLM OPK based at Łęczyca (1st Aerial Defence Corps), 26. PLM OPK based at Zegrze Pomorskie (2nd Air Defence Corps) and 3. PLM OPK based at Wrocław (3rd Air Defence Corps).

On 5 August 1964 13. PLM OPK based at Łęczyca received three MiG-21F-13 aircraft, including two from 1. PLM OPK ("806" and "807"). "2223" arrived from 62. PLM OPK. The fourth MiG-21F-13 ("802") arrived at Łęczyca air base as late as September 1965 after one year of service in the Debrzno regiment. On 8 August 1964 three MiG-21F-13s ("803", "804" and "805") were transferred from 1. PLM OPK to 26. PLM OPK based at Zegrze Pomorskie. Also in August 3. PLM OPK based at Wrocław received four MiG-21F-13 fighters from the Krzesiny regiment ("2017", "2223", "2224" and "2307"). In 1964 MiG-21F-13 aircraft were transferred also to two fighter regiments of Operational Aviation, 40. PLM based at Świdwin and 41. PLM based at Malbork. Four MiG-21F-13 aircraft ("811", "812", "813" and "814") were transferred to Świdwin from 11. PLM based at Debrzno. Three arrived in August ("814" among others) and the fourth one ("811") only after the repair completed in March 1965. In August the Malbork regiment received two MiG-21F-13s from 11. PLM OPK ("808" and "809") and one aircraft ("2019") was transferred from the Air Training Centre at Modlin in November.

In 1965 two crashes of MiG-21F-13 aircraft occurred. The first one happened on 23 June in the 40. PLM based at Świdwin, which was then operating from Goleniów air base. "814" crashed due to engine failure caused by a manufacturing defect and its pilot, 1st Lt Cyryl Królewski was killed. As compensation, one extra MiG-21PFM was delivered from the USSR. The second MiG-21F-13 crash in 1965 took place on 13 October in 13. PLM OPK at Łęczyca. Just after take-off "804" encountered a hydraulic system failure and loss of engine thrust. The pilot managed to turn back towards the base and ejected at an altitude of 100 m, which was too low for the parachute to open. Capt. Eugeniusz Machnicki was killed. The aircraft crashed 7.5 km away from the airfield.

Over the next years 13. PLM at Łęczyca was plagued by less menacing incidents. On 18 August 1966 the pilot of "2015", flying as a wingman, caused a mid-air collision with the for-

130

[130]: MiG-21F-13 "2220" in flight at high altitude.

mation leader, hitting the leader's stabilator with his air data probe. Both fighters returned to base and the damage was repaired. On 5 May 1967 pilot error on landing "2224" caused the aircraft to hit the runway with the ventral fin, damaging it and destroying both main wheel tyres. The aircraft was repaired and returned to service.

In 1965 MiG-21F-13s were withdrawn from service in a further two regiments, 26. PLM OPK based at Zegrze Pomorskie and 3. PLM OPK based at Wrocław. Deliveries of MiG-21PF fighters from June to August 1965 enabled complete re-equipment of squadrons of the regiments based at Wrocław and Zegrze Pomorskie. The airplanes withdrawn from these units were transferred to 13. PLM OPK based at Łęczyca. Deliveries of the PF variants also allowed ordering aircraft inventories of the regiments based at Mińsk Mazowiecki, Debrzno and Krzesiny. The apparent superiority of the MiG-21PF variant then being introduced over the previously operated MiG-21F-13s meant that the commands of both Aerial Defence Forces and Operational Aviation deemed these "deltas", in 1962 fascinating with their speed and modernity, not adequate. The popular old nickname "fast movers" gave way to "old". Thus both commands made attempts to get rid of MiG-21F-13s to replace them with new variants. By April 1966 eleven MiG-21F-13s operated by the Aerial Defence Forces ("802", "803", "804", "805", "806", "807", "2015", "2017", "2223", "2224" and "2307") were concentrated in the 13. PLM OPK, based at Łęczyca, where they remained in service till 1968.

By late October 1966 similar efforts were made by the Operational Aviation and seven F-13s ("808", "809", "811", "812", "813", "2018" and "2019") were grouped in 4. PLM at Goleniów. When in 1966 deliveries of MiG-21PFM variants to Poland began, the dispute as to which units the new aircraft should be assigned and where the MiG-21PFs and F13s should be transferred to was intensified. The MiG-21PFM, apart from the new radar, featured uprated engine, blown flaps and SPS (Russian: *sduv pogranichnego sloya*) boundary layer control (BLC) system. Bleed air from the compressor of the R-11F2S-300 turbojet was blown on the upper surface of the flaps. The air blast on the flaps increased the speed of the boundary layer and prevented flow separation. Increasing the flap deflection angle did not cause any loss of their effectiveness. The boundary layer control system increased lift generated by flaps and improved take-off and landing characteristics. This new feature of the PFM, and the capability of carrying

131

[130–131]: *MiG-21F-13 "2220" rolled out on the flightline. The towbar is used for steering.*

132

twin-barrel 23 mm cannon in a ventral pod, was deemed most useful in the Operational Aviation by its CO, Brig. Gen. Franciszek Kamiński. Brig. Gen. Kamiński proposed that the regiments of the Operational Aviation be equipped with the new MiG-21PFM version, and MiG-21PF and F-13 be concentrated in the Aerial Defence Forces units. The CO of the Aerial Defence Forces, Gen. Czesław Mankiewicz, accepted the takeover of MiG-21PF fighters, but saw no possibility of further use of the troublesome and ineffective MiG-21F-13s.

On 8 March 1967 a fatal crash occurred during a night training sortie in the 4. PLM at Goleniów. The MiG-21F-13 "808", piloted by 1st Lt Paweł Kacprzak, took off tasked with attaining a speed of Mach 1.6 at 13,000 m. One minute after take-off, the aircraft crashed in a forest, breaking trees in a 600 m strip. The pilot made a flying error and was killed.

The Inspectorate of Aviation was considering several possibilities for employment of the MiG-21F-13 fighters, intended for clear weather operations. One was conversion to tactical reconnaissance aircraft. The Czechoslovak Aero Vodochody plant, producing the MiG-21F-13 in the MiG-21FR reconnaissance variant with AFA-39 cameras in underwing pods, offered the conversion. Eventually a solution was found in October 1968, grouping all MiG-21F-13 aircraft in the 2. PLM at Goleniów, where they were classified as reserve aircraft. Three MiG-21F-13s from ATC Modlin ("2007", "2008" and "2009") were so designated, after pilot conversion on this type had been completed.

Before the process of retiring MiG-21F-13 aircraft began in 1973, two were lost in the 2. PLM at Goleniów. MiG-21F-13 "2017" returning to base after a mission on 18 January 1973 suffered a nosewheel strut jammed in the retracted position. Repeated attempts to lower the wheel strut, locked behind closed nosewheel doors, by normal and emergency methods failed. 1st Lt Janusz Rybołowicz decided not to make a belly landing on the emergency grass runway. Having received an order to climb to 2,000 m he reached 5,000 m and ejected. Although the airstream tore off his flying helmet he did not lose consciousness, but manually opened the parachute and survived. Aircraft 2017 crashed in a forest near Niewiadów. It was the only successful ejection from a MiG-21F-13 in Poland.

Capt. Ryszard Krzeszewski was very lucky when landing "803" after a night sortie on 22 June 1973. After the touchdown the left tyre was torn off. The wheel, wing and flap were damaged. After repair the aircraft returned to service.

The fifth and final crash of a MiG-21F-13 took place on 28 August 1973 in the 2. PLM. During a practice aerial fight with the use of R-3U practice missiles, aircraft "813" piloted by 1st Lt Jan Turowski approached very close to the target aircraft. He flew into the exhaust gases of this aircraft, which caused engine flameout in his aircraft. Instead of ejecting, he attempted to restart the engine, but the engine failed to reach proper RPM and the aircraft crashed, killing the pilot.

For nearly two years the MiG-21F-13 fighters were classified as reserve aircraft by the Air Force Command and the sale of these aircraft was taken into consideration. During 1968–1972 the aircraft underwent medium overhauls. The sale of redundant fighters was possible by proxy of *Cenzin* (*Centralny Zarząd Inżynierii*, Central Engineering Executive). When a purchase offer came from Egypt, Polish military authorities proposed sale of 19 aircraft from the Air Force inventory. However, the transaction did not come into effect and the MiG-21F-13s remained at Goleniów in the inventory of 2. PLM. The MiG-21F-13s stood their last Quick Reaction Alert on 13 October 1973. At that time there were 17 aircraft of this type in the inventory of that regiment.

133 *[133]: MiG-21F-13s "2220", "2018" and "2223" at Krzesiny air base.*

In October 1973 a decision was made in Poland to send MiG-21F-13 aircraft to Syria. Twelve were qualified for the transfer (serial numbers 740802, 740803, 740807, 740811, 740812, 742007, 742008 742009, 742018, 742019, 742223 and 742224). They were flown to Powidz, where they were dismantled and prepared for shipment. The entire effort to transfer of the aircraft was top secret, and the only information about it mentioned "a task to be accomplished in the Middle East". The group of personnel participating in the secret deployment, 34 in number, was organized on 16 October. The technical crew of 23 came from the Goleniów regiment and 45. PWL (45. *Polowe Warsztaty Lotnicze* – 45th Field Aircraft Maintenance Depot) based at Malbork. The flight crews comprised three pilots from 2. PLM, Maj. Zbigniew Biedrzycki, Capt. Szymon Krupa and Capt. Czesław Stawski. The mission was so secret that the personnel from 45. PWL had not been informed where they would be sent and why. Taking any personal belongings was forbidden. Every participant in this secret deployment received money for necessary purchases on location. There was also the "assistance" of a counter-intelligence officer and NCO. Other personnel (staying in Poland) disassembled the aircraft at Powidz.

On 18 October six Soviet An-12 four-engine turboprop transport aircraft took four disassembled MiG-21F-13 aircraft, personnel and auxiliary equipment from Powidz. The An-12s were assigned to a transport aviation regiment based in the Lithuanian SSR. As was common in Soviet military aviation, they wore civilian Aeroflot markings. On 20 October the second batch of five An-12s took a further four disassembled aircraft, with spare parts and Polish pilots. On the next day the last four MiG-21F-13s, loaded into four An-12s, departed Powidz air base. The route of the flight to Aleppo airfield in Syria ran over Wrocław and Prague to a Soviet airfield near Budapest. There the aircraft refueled before a further flight, at an altitude of 7,000 m, over Sarajevo, Dubrovnik, the Adriatic Sea and the Ionian Sea, to land in Syria after 6–6.5 hours of flight, having previously bypassed Crete and Cyprus. The MiGs unloaded from the transport aircraft were assembled at the airfield in the open air. During air raid alerts they were quickly pushed into the hangars. From 24 October three Polish pilots test-flew the assembled aircraft. These test flights were considered combat missions, since the Yom Kippur war was in progress. They were flown under threat of an Israeli air raid on the airfield and nearby area. Therefore the aircraft were armed with R-3S missiles and cannon ammunition was loaded. Polish pilots were ordered to fight in case of encountering Israeli fighters. However, there was no such situation. After the test flights were completed the aircraft underwent routine maintenance, were armed and, after the installation of the external tanks, they went to the paint shop to have Syrian markings and camouflage applied. The last aircraft test-flown was serial number 740803. After the test flight and application of camouflage fuel leaks were revealed on the port wing in the rivet joints. This could have resulted from damage sustained during disassembly or transport. A wing replacement was ordered. A Polish An-12 from 13th Transport Regiment based at Cracow brought in another pair of wings. After the replacement of the wings and two test flights, made by Maj. Biedrzycki, 740803 was cleared for operations. Like other ex-Polish fighters it was ferried to front-line unit by a Soviet pilot in Syrian uniform. The further fate of the twelve MiG-21F-13 aircraft in the Syrian Air Force after the transfer from Poland is not known.

The Polish Air Force lost seven MiG-21F-13 aircraft due to failures and crashes. Some survived as museum exhibits.

"1217" found its way to Hermeskeil, West Germany, where it is displayed without Polish markings. Remaining in Poland are

134

135

[134–136]: MiG-21F-13 "2223" at Goleniów airfield. SK-1 ejection seat is being maintained with the use of the crane.

136

137

[137]: Preflight maintenance of "2223" at Goleniów airfield. The aircraft is connected to a truck-mounted ground power unit. The air data probe and air intake are covered.

138

[138]: Small wing fences are mounted on the upper wing surfaces and on the lower surfaces are RV-2 radar altimeter antennas. NR-30 cannon muzzle is located on the lower starboard side.

[139]: MiG-21F-13 aircraft "2015" and "2224". These aircraft were damaged during service in 13. PLM at Łęczyca, but after repairs returned to service.

139

140

[140]: MiG-21F-13 "2307" on display at Lubuskie Military Muzeum in Drzonów. This aircraft was delivered to Poland on 11 January 1963. After service in four regiments: 62. PLM, 3. PLM, 13. PLM and 2. PLM, it was transferred to COSSTWL technical school in Oleśnica and then to Drzonów museum.

141

142

[141]: MiG-21F-13 "802" takes off with a training missile mounted under the port wing. It was initially operated by 1. PLM "Warszawa". Upon completing service in 2. PLM it was sold to Syria and sent there in October 1973.

[142]: MiG-21F-13 "802". Note the thin rim of the supersonic air intake and the movable air data probe mount.

"2015", preserved at the Polish Air Force Museum in Dęblin, "2307" at Lubuskie Military Museum in Drzonów, "806" at a military base in Sklęczki and "809" at the Polish Aviation Museum in Cracow.

The graceful silhouette of the MiG-21F-13 with its sleek fuselage and vertical fin is impressive. It is hard to disagree that its shape gave it a subtle beauty, not repeated in the later versions. In the opinion of pilots who flew it, the MiG-21F-13 had the best flying characteristics in comparison with all subsequent variants of this family. It was the lightest and most agile of them all. According to Gen. Tytus Krawczyc, it could easily make vertical flight maneuvers without the afterburner engaged, which was not possible with subsequent versions, e.g. MiG-21R or MiG-21M.

143

[143]: MiG-21F-13 "802" on the flightline at Goleniów airfield.

[144]: MiG-21F-13 "803" taking off from Goleniów airfield in August 1970. It commenced service in 1. PLM "Warszawa" after being delivered on 14 September 1963. During service in 2. PLM it was damaged in 1973. After repair it flew until the end of service of this version in Goleniów and then was sold to Syria.

144

145

[145]: . MiG-21F-13 "804" assigned to 1. PLM "Warszawa". It was lost in a crash on 13 October 1965, when assigned to 13. PLM based at Łęczyca.

146

[146]: MiG-21F-13 "805". The aircraft has no checkerboard on the fuselage.

147

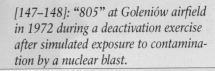

[147–148]: "805" at Goleniów airfield in 1972 during a deactivation exercise after simulated exposure to contamination by a nuclear blast.

148

[149]: MiG-21F-13 "806" preserved at Sklęczki military base, photographed by Roman Kopras.

149

[150]: MiG-21F-13 "806". Its first unit was 1. PLM "Warszawa" from 14 September 1963.

150

[151]: MiG-21F-13s "807" and "2224" at the airfield of 2. PLM in Goleniów. Both aircraft were sold to Syria.

151

[152]: MiG-21F-13 "807" on approach to landing. Note the lack of a checkerboard on the fuselage.

152

153

154

[153–154]: MiG-21F-13 "809" photographed by Wacław Hołyś after being withdrawn from service on the airfield of COSSTWL technical school in Oleśnica. From 16 September 1963 it was operated by 11. PLM at Debrzno. Then it was transferred to 41. PLM at Malbork and 4. PLM at Goleniów. It was not sold to Syria, but instead was transferred to Oleśnica and then to Cracow museum.

[155]: MiG-21F-13 "809" displayed at Polish Aviation Museum in Cracow, photographed by Jacek Jazgar.

155

156

157

[157]: "813" with flaps lowered prior to take-off.

[156]: MiG-21F-13 "813" – one of last two aircraft of this version delivered to Poland. It remained in service for 10 years and was lost in a crash on 28 August 1973 in 2. PLM "Kraków".

158

[158]: "813" in inverted flight.

159

[159]: "813" photographed in flight. Checkerboards on lower wing surfaces have incorrect colour sequence .

[160]: „813" with flaps in take-off position just after liftoff.

160

[161]: MiG-21F-13 "813" 2 PLM "Kraków", in natural metal finish. The ailerons and wing panels over the fuel tanks differ in gloss and shade of the duralumin. Green panels on the wings house SOD-57M transponder antennas. The checkerboards on lower wing surfaces have incorrect colour sequence.

161

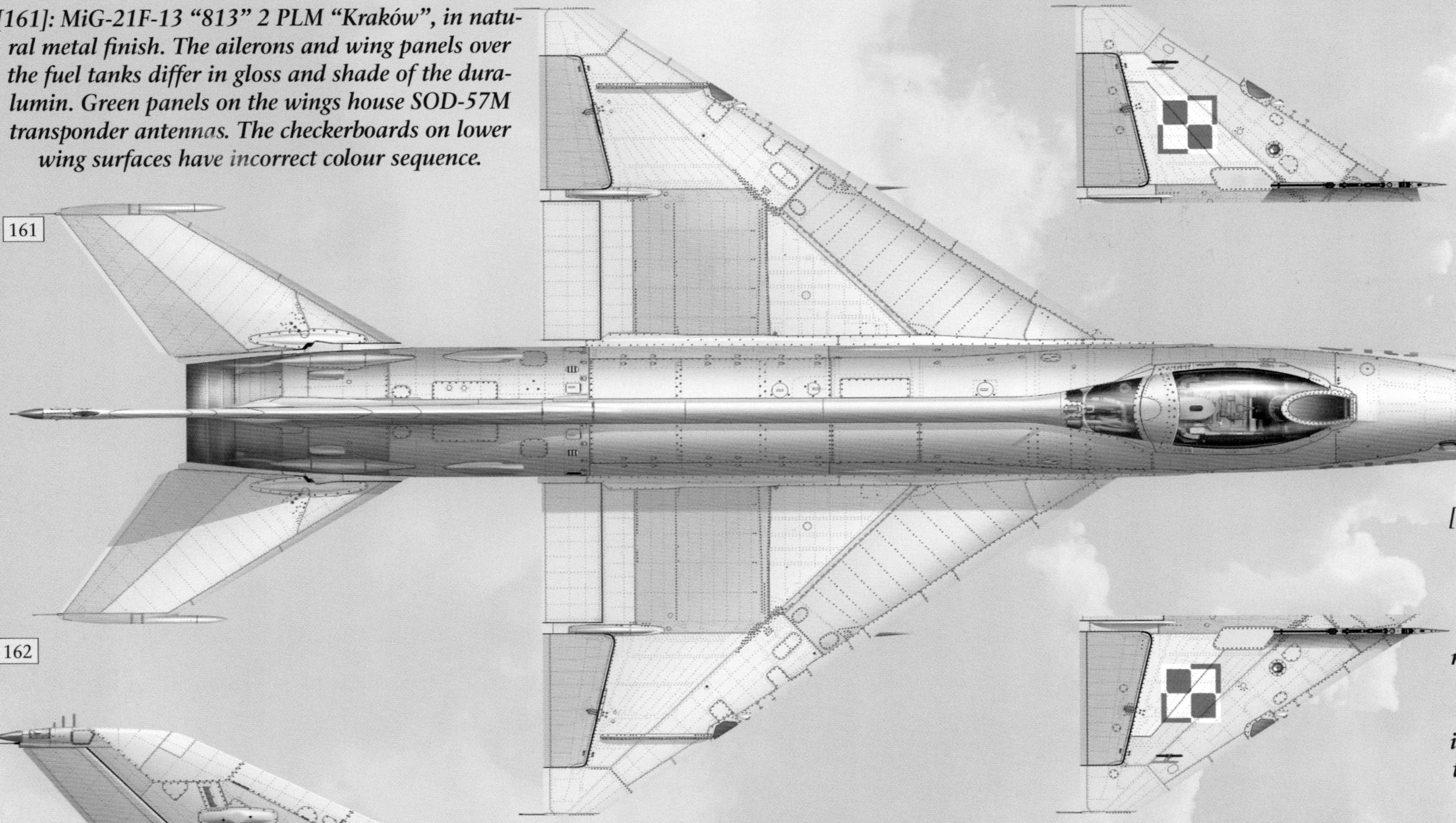

162

[162]: MiG-21F-13 "813". Green fairings house the following antennas: "Lazur" datalink in the ventral fin, MRP-56P marker beacon receiver on lower fuselage above the fin, Sirena-2 radar warning receiver and SOD-57M transponder on the side of the vertical stabilizer.

163

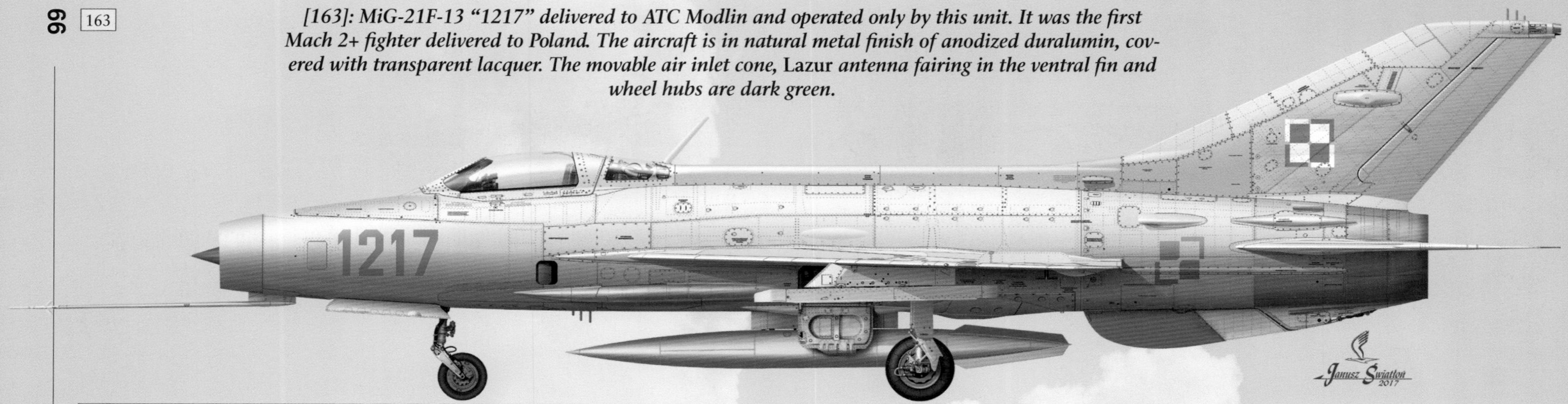

[163]: MiG-21F-13 "1217" delivered to ATC Modlin and operated only by this unit. It was the first Mach 2+ fighter delivered to Poland. The aircraft is in natural metal finish of anodized duralumin, covered with transparent lacquer. The movable air inlet cone, Lazur *antenna fairing in the ventral fin and wheel hubs are dark green.*

164 *[164]: The first MiG-21F-13 delivered to Modlin. It landed there on 29 June 1961.*

165

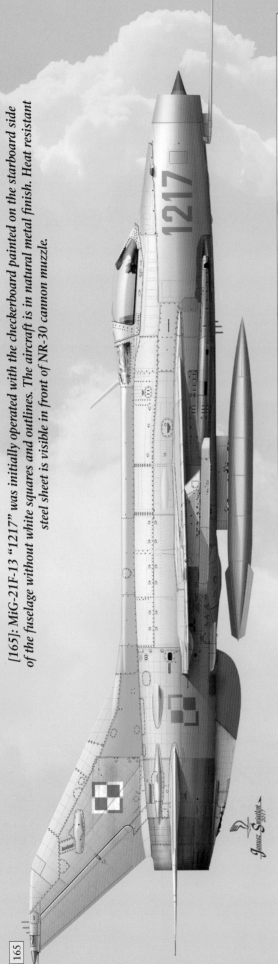

[165]: MiG-21F-13 "1217" was initially operated with the checkerboard painted on the starboard side of the fuselage without white squares and outlines. The aircraft is in natural metal finish. Heat resistant steel sheet is visible in front of NR-30 cannon muzzle.

166

[166]: One of the first photographs of the first MiG-21F-13 "1217" delivered to Poland. Skin panels of various shades are visible on the aircraft, painted only with transparent lacquer. The engine air intake is closed with a red cover, with aircraft tactical number.

167

[167]: MiG-21F-13 "1217" being prepared for towing at Modlin airfield. Ground crews attach the towbar to the nosewheel and towing lines to the main landing gear struts.

168

[168]: MiG-21F-13 "2017" from 2. PLM "Kraków" based at Goleniów carrying R-3S air-to-air guided missiles under the wings. The aircraft is in natural metal finish of anodized duralumin, covered with transparent lacquer.

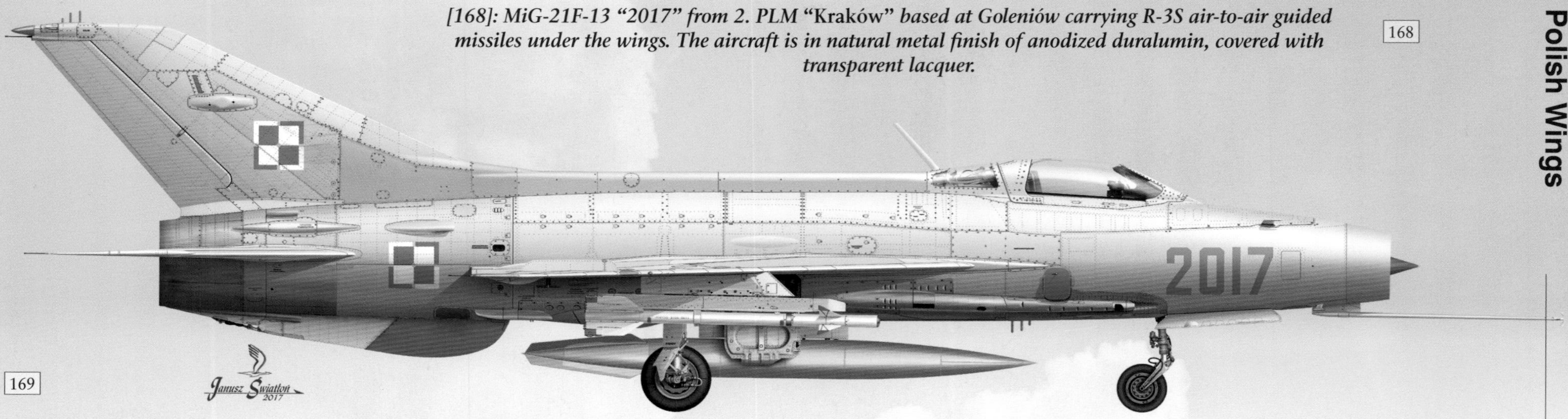

169

[169]: MiG-21F-13 "2017" from 2. PLM "Kraków" at Goleniów airfield, armed with two R-3S (K-13) air-to-air guided missiles. The aircraft is connected to an APA-5 ground power unit mounted on a Ural-375 truck.

170

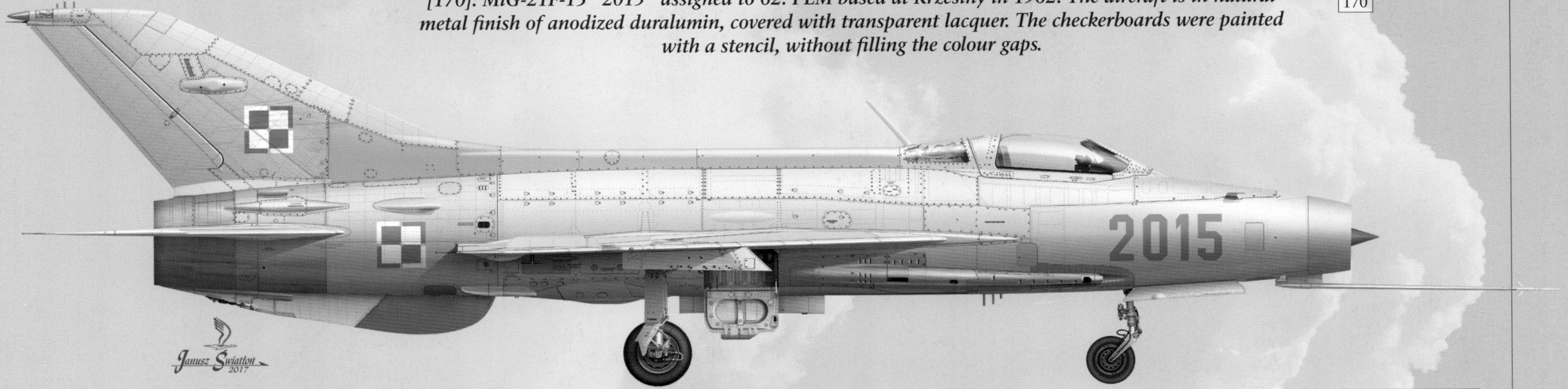

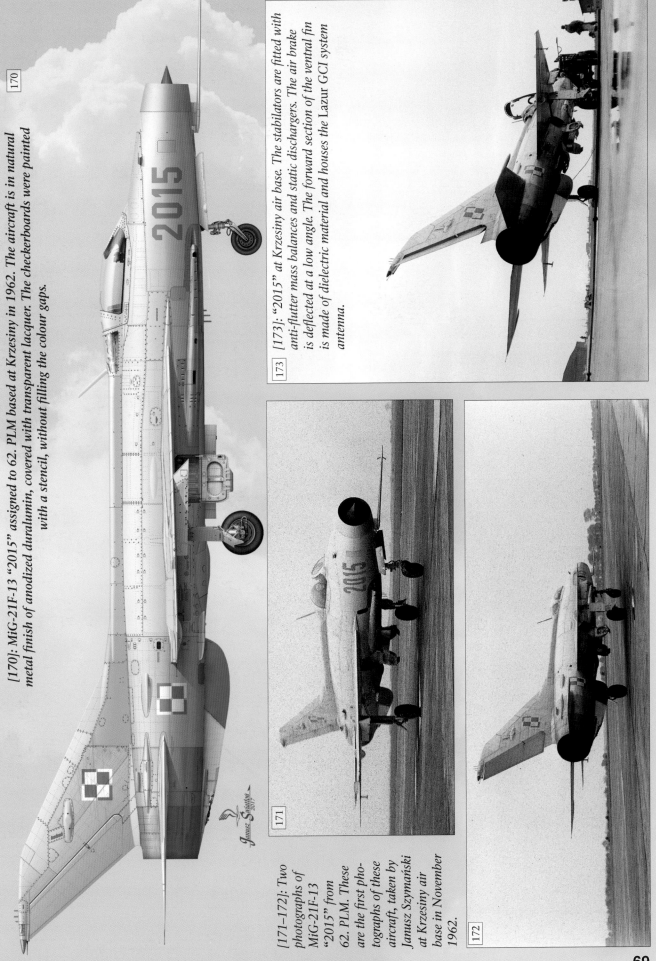

[170]: MiG-21F-13 "2015" assigned to 62. PLM based at Krzesiny in 1962. The aircraft is in natural metal finish of anodized duralumin, covered with transparent lacquer. The checkerboards were painted with a stencil, without filling the colour gaps.

171

172

[171–172]: Two photographs of MiG-21F-13 "2015" from 62. PLM. These are the first photographs of these aircraft, taken by Janusz Szymański at Krzesiny air base in November 1962.

173

[173]: "2015" at Krzesiny air base. The stabilators are fitted with anti-flutter mass balances and static dischargers. The air brake is deflected at a low angle. The forward section of the ventral fin is made of dielectric material and houses the Lazur GCI system antenna.

174

[174]: Following retirement MiG-21F-13 "2015", serial number 742015, received a multi-colour camouflage, when in the late1960s/early1970s various camouflage patterns for aircraft were tested.

175

dark olive green (C71/M26/Y63/K51)

dark green (C78/M23/Y42/K32)

light green (C44/M17/Y58/K12)

green-grey (C55/M13/Y29/K12)

light blue (C56/M7/Y0/K1)

[175]: MiG-21F-13 "2015" in camouflage applied after retirement. Photo taken in 1993.

176

[176–177]: MiG-21F-13 "2015". Camouflage pattern and colours as of 1993: olive green, dark green, light green, green-grey and light blue. Estimated colors according to CMYK colour model are shown on the previous page. The starboard wing flap is in natural metal finish. The inlet cone and weapon pylon tips are red. The tactical number is white (height – 32.5 cm, width of the entire number – 96 cm, gaps between digits – 11 cm). A non-standard paint scheme using non-standard colours.

177

Janusz Świątłoń 2017

178

[178]: MiG-21F-13 "811" from 2. PLM "Kraków", carrying two UB-16-57U launchers with sixteen 57 mm S-5 unguided rockets each. No fuselage checkerboard.

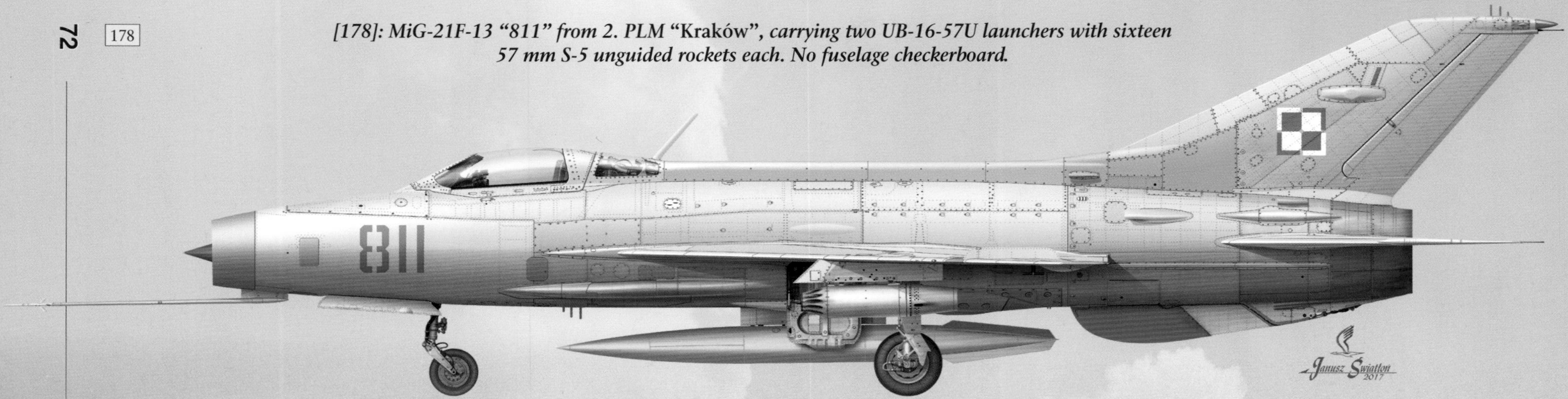

179

[179]: MiG-21F-13 "811" in 2. PLM "Kraków". Note the digit "8" painted with a stencil with wide gaps. The pilot, second from left, is Maj. Zbigniew Biedrzycki. In October 1973, along with two other pilots of 2. PLM, Capts. Czesław Stawski and Szymon Krupa, he test flew MiG-21F-13 aircraft delivered to Syria at Syrian Aleppo airfield. He made the test flights in "803", "2009", "2018" and "2223".

[180]: MiG-21F-13 lands at Goleniów, with brake chute deployed. The pitching moment, pressing the nosewheel to the runway and increasing braking effectiveness, is visible. This aircraft was transferred to Syria.

180